Brief Points

An Almanac for Parents and Friends
of U.S. Naval Academy Midshipmen

THIRD EDITION

Ross H. Mackenzie

Naval Institute Press
Annapolis, Maryland

Naval Institute Press
291 Wood Road
Annapolis, MD 21402

Library of Congress Cataloging-in-Publication Data

Mackenzie Ross, H., 1971–
    Brief points : an almanac for parents and friends of U.S. Naval Academy midshipmen / Ross H. Mackenzie.— 3rd ed.
      p. cm.
    Includes index.
    ISBN-10: 1-59114-506-6 (pbk.:alk.paper)
    ISBN-13: 978-1-59114-506-6 (pbk.:alk.paper)
    1. United States Naval Academy. I. Title.
    V415.P1 M33 2004
    359'.0071'173—dc22

                                                    2003024027

Printed in the United States of America on acid-free paper ∞
11 10 09   9 8 7 6 5 4 3

Contents

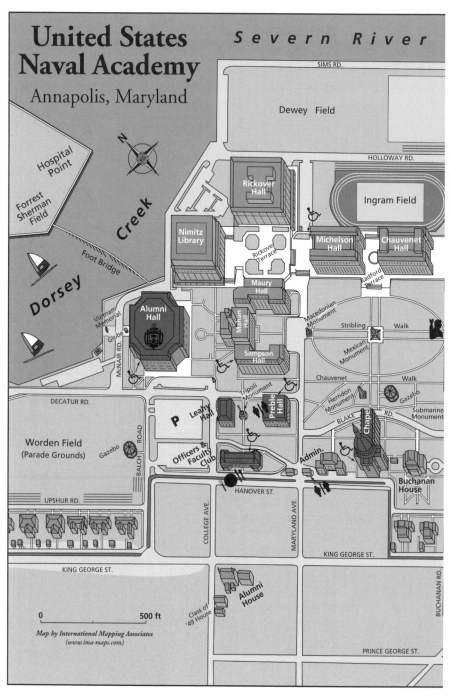

Map of U.S. Naval Academy
© Alex Tait at International Mapping Associates

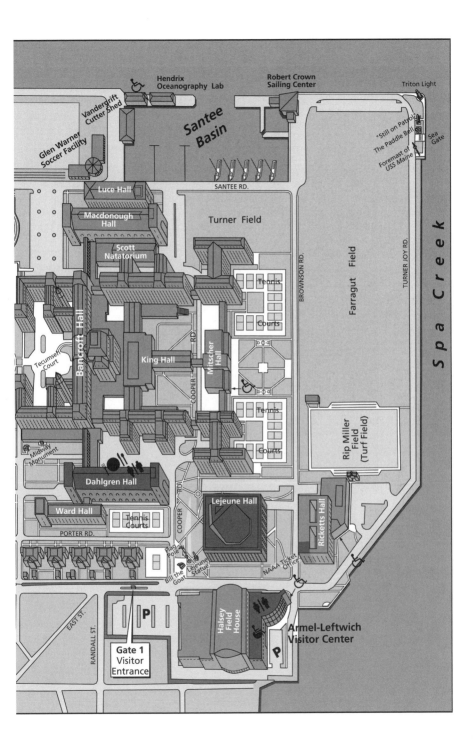

Ross H. Mackenzie (in shirt with happy face) atop classmates at his Herndon ceremony.

Courtesy of Andrea Mackenzie

Preface

You are probably looking at this book because you want to learn more about the U.S. Naval Academy in Annapolis, Maryland, and the midshipmen who attend it. My goal is to tell you just that. I hope to provide a user-friendly introduction and guide for all individuals interested in learning about the Academy's fundamental facts, nuances, modus operandi, and unique language. To my knowledge, no other book covers this topic so fully in terms of scope and details.

Earlier editions of *Brief Points: An Almanac for Parents and Friends of U.S. Naval Academy Midshipmen* succeeded in achieving my same primary goal, but many things have changed in the last decade—both within the gates of the Naval Academy Yard and beyond. How the Naval Academy operates also has been affected by world events. This current edition reflects the changes in a clear fashion while it also directs people seeking more knowledge to other appropriate—primarily online—sources.

Two significant changes have occurred since the second edition of *Brief Points* was published in 1996. First, the Internet was in its infancy at that time. Today most people are familiar with the World Wide Web, although many experience frustration while navigating through the endless supply of information available. Much of the information covered in this edition of *Brief Points* is also available online somewhere, but not in one easy-to-find spot. The goals of this edition, therefore, are twofold: first, to provide the fundamental facts of the school (as the first two editions did) and to direct readers to appropriate Web sites—many of which are the Academy's own—for further specifics. The appendix lists the major Internet resources mentioned. Second, philologists state that languages constantly change. The Naval Academy's language, called "Midspeak," is no different. This edition of *Brief Points* provides an ambitiously expanded and improved dictionary of Midspeak that reflects language changes. Definitions are clearly presented and, when needed, examples are provided to illustrate proper usage.

My experience with the Academy made me eager to take a leading role in updating this book. My experience there provided me with the credentials necessary to do the job properly. I graduated from the Academy and I was a varsity athlete. I taught English literature and writing at the Academy for three years and served as an Officer Representative for a varsity sports team. My familiarity and an eye into the school give me something that the previous author—my father—could never possess because he was not a student at the Academy himself. He explained in an earlier edition of *Brief Points*, "Possibly, even probably, no one can understand [the Naval Academy] until he or she has been aboard a while." While I *have* been aboard a while, I should emphasize here that the views presented in these pages are mine and not necessarily those of the Department of Defense or its components.

The process of updating *Brief Points* was far from a solitary one. With the help of the Academy's public affairs office, I interviewed midshipmen, faculty, and staff, picking their brains for minute details of the place and repeatedly revisiting them to ensure my facts were correct. The USNA photo lab provided photographs beautifully illustrating the Academy and its people as it exists today. The Superintendent has called the Academy "one of the premier colleges in the world"; the Dean has called it the world's "most highly selective university." The Academy ranks among the top colleges anywhere. It has an incredibly challenging curriculum. In seeking to train midshipmen "morally, mentally, and physically," the Academy provides an experience uniquely different from any offered by the nation's civilian colleges. It also is different from its sister military academies.

The Naval Academy is also not for everyone. As you will learn in the following pages, the Academy combines an incredibly demanding academic regimen with a traditional military regimen, all the while including requirements in physical training, athletics, and professional development. The end result affects each midshipman differently. Some thrive; others, although equally intelligent and gifted, do not.

While midshipmen attempt to sort out myriad Academy requirements, they also spend a great deal of time attempting to sort themselves out as well. For many, "The Academy is a horrible place to *be,* but a fantastic place to be *from.*" No matter what their midshipmen children may tell them during their years at the Academy, most parents believe that the Academy is the most wonderful place on earth. It may be just that, but to many midshipmen existing within its confines or clutches, the Academy seems anything but wonderful. While a few will sail through the Academy years loving every minute, many more will come to know the true meaning of self-doubt and self-esteem. Some midshipmen will doubt their decision to attend the Academy; some will want to leave; some will get in trouble; some will do poorly on tests and papers. All will have periodic bad days. Few midshipmen will believe that their parents and friends can understand their particular predicament or perceived plight. Most will require all the understanding and encouragement those who love and support them can muster. It is imperative that both midshipmen and their parents keep smiling, even during the difficult times.

After graduation, however, the story changes. Many begin to believe that the Academy affords young men and women opportunities impossible to obtain through other avenues. Many consider a military career to be one of the best career choices possible in our country. Many argue that the combination of a top-notch education and a guaranteed job following graduation in any number of remarkable fields of expertise is something so wonderful that the positives awaiting graduates vastly outweigh any perceived or actual negatives encountered as a midshipman. I believe this last statement to be true, even admitting that I certainly did not enjoy every minute of my Academy years. It is imperative, therefore, that parents and friends of midshipmen know as much about a midshipman's experience as possible. That's the reason for this book. It's a guide. A handbook. A reference to turn to when nothing else seems to help.

I have done my best to simply provide facts. Period. *Brief Points,* whose title purposely mimics the annually published plebe information manual called *Reef Points,* is not concerned with philosophy but rather with certainty—not with whys but rather with whats. Personal beliefs are not important. What matters are the facts, stated in an unbiased manner. Prior to reading the text, however, a few subjects are important to stress here.

Consistency: No two Naval Academy experiences are the same. While all midshipmen have many things in common, each individual is unique. Furthermore, each company is different, each with its own Company Officer. While each midshipman is held responsible for his or her actions under the midshipmen regulations, each company has varying regulations as well as various enforcement policies. Certain actions or policies that one midshipman may gripe about may not be an issue for another midshipman.

Security: Our world is a very different place than it was in 1996 when the second edition of *Brief Points* was published. Our world will likely continue to change. With each change, the Naval Academy works passionately and diligently to update its security procedures and precautions in an effort to protect midshipmen. The fluid nature of these procedures at times may aggravate parents and other visitors, but be assured that security precautions exist as a real barrier between potential threats and the midshipmen you care so much about.

Support: Most midshipmen, whether they admit it or not, draw an incredible amount of strength from familial support. As loved ones, your response to midshipman emotion is critical. The Academy acknowledges the maturity of midshipmen as soon-to-be officers; they, therefore, are treated like adults. Parents, even though they are your children, they are adults. Adults—like everyone—need advice. I recommend that you give your best advice to your respective midshipman. But adults also must make decisions. When a decision is made by your adult midshipman, I recommend that you support it, whether it is a decision to leave the Academy, a decision to become something you deem too dangerous such as a pilot or SEAL, or any other decision made during a midshipman's Academy years. Never forget the importance your opinion and advice carries as a parent, but similarly never forget the significance your support and understanding mean to your child.

And understanding is what this book is all about.

Acknowledgments

The production of the third edition of *Brief Points* was a collective effort. Although my name appears on the cover, I would be remiss not to mention people who helped make it a reality.

Midshipmen: David Blossom, Darrin Briggs, Joe Doman, Graham Gill, Kristyn Kern, Carl Lepard, Jason Mortimer, Steph Parker, Adam Sipp, Eduardo Vargas, Greg Woelfel, Alan Zarracina, Bethany Zmitrovich, and dozens of others who chose not to be named

USNA Faculty and Staff: Mike Andrews, Matt Bonzella, Jeanne Chatelain, Greg Cotton, Fred Davis, Katie Dooley, Diane Green, Mike Hurni, Ben Johnson, Jo Jones, Blair Kiethley, Rick Klauer, Bob Madison, Jeff Melody, Sharon Moffatt, Steve Morganfeld, Matthew Phelps, Tony Porter, Tom Sheppard, Mark Smith, Bill Spann, Matthew Tritle, Maureen Tyson, Laurie Wells, USNA public affairs office, USNA photo lab

Miscellaneous: Kathleen Barnes, Katie Brill, Robb Jolley, Andrea Mackenzie, Elizabeth Mackenzie, Ross D. Mackenzie, Stuart W. Mackenzie, Matthew Provencher, Mike Provencher, Kathy Sandoz, Anne Sharpe, U.S. Naval Institute Press staff, Mike and Sandi Zets

There are certainly names missing from the above list; for that I apologize. I wish to say thank you to everyone who helped for their dedication to this project, their patience, and their determination to help me get the most accurate information possible.

Brief Points

–1–

Profile and Admissions

Profile

Midshipmen come in all shapes and sizes, both sexes, and of more colors than a box of crayons. Their roads to the U.S. Naval Academy (USNA) in Annapolis, Maryland, vary; some are pot-holed and others are well paved. But the young men and women arrive nevertheless. While unique in their own ways, they do possess certain similarities.

On Induction Day (I-Day), they must be at least seventeen years old but not older than twenty-two. High school and preadmission records show most midshipmen to be hard working, high achieving, and persevering young men and women. The Academy says they are also well

A midshipman officer keeps her "eyes in the boat" during a formal parade. *Courtesy of USNA*

rounded. About 80 percent of those entering from high school stand academically in the top 20 percent of their graduating class. They arrive bristling—some bristling more than others—with academic, athletic, and extracurricular awards. More so than most of their high school peers, they appear disciplined and focused.

During their years in the Academy's never-changing, ever-changing microcosm, they will experience common suffering in a harsh regimen. They will come to hate drill and to dread the Dark Ages (the period between January and spring break). They will long for liberty and loathe the Hall (the common term for Bancroft Hall). They will log countless hours on room telephones or mobile phones (an upperclass privilege), desperately trying to get girlfriends, boyfriends, and loved ones to understand their inexpressible plight.

And regardless of what you, as a parent or friend, may think they are experiencing, and regardless of what they may tell you, many will not enjoy their Academy years.

Yet after these four years of sometimes-perceived torment and myopia, the young men and women will emerge vastly more mature than when they entered. They will be steeped in learning, leadership, and professionalism. Some will never want to look back; others will look forward to their first reunion with glee. But each graduate (that is, each complete participant of this place) emerges with an uncommon esprit and an invaluable shared experience. If nothing else, their experience at the Academy helps prepare these young men and women extraordinarily for future endeavors, both military and civilian.

Law mandates that there be midshipmen in each year's class from each of the fifty states. While the numbers of appointments vary from year to year, the geographical distribution for a typical year is shown in table 1. The current chart of geographical distribution is printed each year in the *United States Naval Academy Catalog;* it is also available at www.usna.edu/Catalog, along with the current plebe (equivalent to a freshman at a civilian college) class profile.

In addition, for the particular year shown, there were also fourteen midshipmen from U.S. territories (Guam, Puerto Rico, and the Virgin Islands) and thirty-two from nineteen foreign countries.

Admissions

The Naval Academy is a hugely remarkable, incredibly commendable place. But it is different! Its collegiate experience is vastly different from any offered by civilian colleges. Prospective applicants should enter the admissions process only if they are relatively certain the Naval Academy is what they really want. Following induction, that decision may be questioned many times.

Table 1. Geographical Distribution of Midshipmen

State	Number	State	Number
Alabama	30	Montana	11
Alaska	13	Nebraska	20
Arizona	60	Nevada	24
Arkansas	14	New Hampshire	30
California	422	New Jersey	179
Colorado	59	New Mexico	27
Connecticut	59	New York	262
Delaware	23	North Carolina	99
District of Columbia	9	North Dakota	12
Florida	243	Ohio	138
Georgia	103	Oklahoma	42
Hawaii	21	Oregon	29
Idaho	21	Pennsylvania	276
Illinois	138	Rhode Island	64
Indiana	55	South Carolina	80
Iowa	25	South Dakota	11
Kansas	41	Tennessee	55
Kentucky	34	Texas	354
Louisiana	53	Utah	17
Maine	14	Vermont	9
Maryland	276	Virginia	249
Massachusetts	85	Washington	85
Michigan	76	West Virginia	25
Minnesota	45	Wisconsin	64
Mississippi	18	Wyoming	13
Missouri	51		

While the roads to admission to the Naval Academy begin in many different places, all applicants require two parts of an admissions ticket: approval by the Academy's Admissions Board, and a nomination, which is usually given by a senator or congressman. No one political representative may have nominated more than five incumbent appointees at each military college—the U.S. Naval Academy; the U.S. Air Force Academy in Colorado Springs, Colorado; West Point in Highland Falls, New York; and the Merchant Marine Academy in King's Point (Long Island), New York—at any one time. Although congressional and senatorial nominations are the standard, there do exist many other sources for nominations. For a complete list, visit www.usna.edu/Admissions/steps4.htm.

Midshipmen salute the American flag during an Army-Navy football game.
Courtesy of USNA

Some applicants receive approval by the Admissions Board but do not receive a politician's nomination. Many receive a politician's nomination but do not receive approval by the Admissions Board. Politicians usually nominate ten applicants for each vacancy. Except when a politician makes one of his ten a "principal" nominee, the Academy usually picks the nominees it wants from the pool of qualified nominees and alternates. With both parts of the admissions ticket punched, applicants can then compete with other fully qualified applicants for offers of appointment.

While all applicants require two parts of an admissions ticket, there do exist some applicants who stay a few steps ahead of others during the admissions process. For example, heavily recruited athletes who are considered "blue chips" are so well qualified in their particular sport that their competition for Admissions Board approval and political nominations differs slightly, tipping the scale in their favor for acceptance. Additionally, the Academy does not have quotas for minorities, but does admit to having an "aggressive outreach program" to reach some ethnic minorities in an attempt to have the student body visually represent the

U.S. Navy's officer corps. In theory, at least, the Navy tries to maintain its officer corps in relation to its enlisted corps.

The Academy has what is considered a rolling admissions process. Those who submit their completed applications and related material early may hear early about their disposition by the Admissions Board. In October the Academy begins offering appointments and letters of assurance. The letters guarantee an applicant's appointment upon his or her receipt of a politician's nomination. The admissions process is completed by mid-May of the following year.

I have sat in the shadows during an actual Admissions Board's deliberation of applicants. It's incredible, to say the least. Everything about a particular applicant usually is presented in approximately two minutes; a few applicants may receive up to twenty minutes of attention. Voting members make their decisions shortly thereafter. The room has an enormous wooden table around which the eighteen board members sit. Stacks of applicant files are piled high. Colored sticks are used to vote while projector screens periodically illustrate amplifying information about a candidate. The board's meeting room is decorated with photographs of

New plebes take their oath of office on Induction Day (I-Day).
Courtesy of USNA

midshipmen engaged in every kind of Academy endeavor, perhaps serving as reminders of who the accepted applicants will become. Officers come and go; they carry new stacks of files to present to the board. The board's task is daunting, incredibly complex, and not open to the public. That said, a tremendous amount of information somehow exists about the Naval Academy's admissions processes; a fair number of books have even been written that claim to help one's chances at being accepted. My goal—and the goal of this book—is *not* to guide hopeful candidates in their search for an appointment. Rather, I will attempt to steer you to the most accurate information of which I am aware. What you do with that information is up to you. Incidentally, most of the information printed here about admissions is also printed in each year's USNA catalog, which is available at www.usna.edu/Catalog.

The average size of the entire Naval Academy's student body—the Brigade—is about forty-four hundred. Although these numbers change on almost a daily basis, a typical year's application data follows:

Total applicants: 12,331 (this number has steadily risen over the last five years)
Total applicants with nomination: 4,200
Total applicants found fully qualified academically, medically, and physically: 1,776
Total offers of admission: 1,457
Total admitted: 1,214

The USNA admissions department currently uses the following table for Scholastic Aptitude Test (SAT) and American College Test (ACT) scores. (See table 2.)
    Other interesting admittance data include:

Midshipmen entering from college or post–high school preparation experience: approximately one-third of all applicants

Table 2. SAT and ACT Score Ranges for USNA Admissions

SAT (ACT) Score Ranges	Verbal (% Mids)	Math (% Mids)
>700 (31–36)	18	31
600-699 (26–30)	56	55
<600 (<26)	26	14

Midshipmen entering with at least six months of college: 50
Midshipmen entering from the Naval Academy Prep School (NAPS): 230
Midshipmen entering from private preparatory schools under sponsorship of the U.S. Naval Academy Foundation, Inc.: 75
Midshipmen entering directly from the fleet: 50 (40 USN, 10 USMC)
Average number of African Americans entering: 86
Average number of Asian Americans entering: 47
Average number of Hispanic Americans entering: 121
Average number of Hawaiian/Pacific Islanders entering: 21
Average number of Native Americans entering: 32
Average number of minorities (total) entering: 300
Average number of women entering: 192
Average number of alumni children entering: 50

Table 3 shows other criteria that may be used by the admissions office. It delineates high school honors and activities of Academy midshipmen.

Table 3. School Honors and Activities of Entering Midshipmen

School Honors and Activities	% Midshipmen
Student government president or vice president	8
Class president or vice president	11
School club president or vice president	26
School publication staff	24
National Honor Society	58
Varsity athletics	86
Varsity letter winners	82
Dramatics, public speaking, or debate	86
Leader of musical group	9
Eagle Scout or Gold Award	11
Boys or Girls State or Nation	17
Reserve officer training programs	11
Sea cadets	3

-2-

Academics

Midshipmen practice their skills in an electrical engineering laboratory.
Courtesy of USNA

The Naval Academy's academic program ranks among the nation's toughest. It is driven by a core curriculum consisting of required courses in engineering, the natural sciences, mathematics, humanities, social sciences, and professional naval courses. When asked, the Academic Dean's office acknowledges the primary technical nature of academics at the Academy. For this reason, *all* graduating midshipmen—whatever their major—receive a Bachelor of Science degree upon graduation.

Overall, the curriculum is highly structured. Throughout much of the Academy's history, midshipmen could not choose their courses. In 1959, the Academy inaugurated electives; in 1969 it converted to a system of majors. Although about half the plebes begin the academic year with some form of advanced placement or Academy validation in one or more courses, they have almost no choice regarding the courses they take. In rare cases they may be eligible to select one elective. Choice, specifically

8

regarding electives and courses in the selected major, increases as midshipmen progress toward graduation. The Academy offers about three hundred courses per semester. The course listing can be viewed at the Academic Dean's Web site (www.usna.edu/acdean/courses/courses.html). In fact, a wealth of information awaits you at www.usna.edu/acdean. It is regularly updated. It also clearly indicates which information is open to the public and which data are restricted to "USNA only" use.

Majors and Divisions

Plebes select one of nineteen majors in their second semester. Depending on the chosen major, a midshipman must take anywhere from thirty to forty-five credit hours in his or her major. The majors are:

Aerospace engineering	Mathematics
Chemistry	Mechanical engineering
Computer science	Naval architecture
Economics	Ocean engineering
Electrical engineering	Oceanography
English	Physics
General engineering	Political science
General science	Quantitative economics
History	Systems engineering
Information technology	

Academic Organization

The Academy has three primary academic divisions: Engineering and Weapons, Mathematics and Science, and Humanities and Social Sciences. It also has a fourth division: Professional Development.

The Division of Engineering and Weapons, comprised of five departments, offers seven majors:

Aerospace engineering	Naval architecture
Electrical engineering	Ocean engineering
General engineering	Systems engineering
Mechanical engineering	

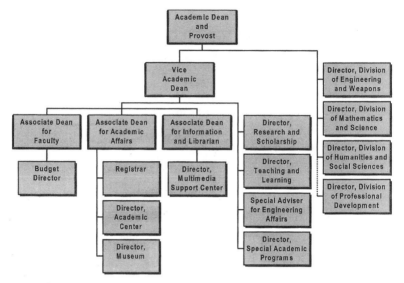

Chart of academic organization at the U.S. Naval Academy.
Courtesy of Fredrick Davis

Midshipmen in any of those seven majors—called group I majors—constitute about 40 percent of the Academy's upperclass. Non–group I majors must take twenty to twenty-three hours of core courses in this division (among them: electrical engineering, thermodynamics, ship structure and performance, and control systems). The "Division of Engineering and Weapons Majors" chart outlines a generic course matrix for group I majors.

The Division of Mathematics and Science, comprised of five departments, offers eight majors:

Chemistry	Mathematics
Computer science	Oceanography
General science	Physics
Information technology	Quantitative economics

Midshipmen in any of those eight majors—called group II majors—constitute about 25 percent of the Academy's upperclass. Courses in this division make up the largest segment of courses in the core curriculum (chemistry, physics, calculus, to name just a few). For this reason, the mathematics department is the largest of the Academy's academic departments. The "Division of Mathematics and Science Majors" chart outlines a generic course matrix for group II majors.

Division of Engineering and Weapons Majors

	4/C		3/C		2/C		1/C	
	Fall	Spring	Fall	Spring	Fall	Spring	Fall	Spring
C O R E	Leadership	Naval Science	Navigation	Ethics	Tactics	Leadership	Law for JO	JO Practicum
	Chemistry1	Chemistry2	Physics1	Physics2	EE1	EE2		
	Calculus1	Calculus2	Calculus3	Differential Equations		Intro Weapons	Wpns & Systems Eng	
	English1	English2	WestCiv1	WestCiv2				
	Naval Heritage	US Gov & Constitution			Humanities SocSci Elctv			Humanities SocSci Elctv
D I V								
M A J O R			Major Course	Major Course	Major Course	Major Course	Major Course	Major Course
			Major Course	Major Course	Major Course	Major Course	Major Course	Major Course
					Major Course	Major Course	Major Course	Major Course
							Major Course	Major Course

A generic course matrix for group I majors at the U.S. Naval Academy.
Courtesy of Fredrick Davis

Division of Mathematics and Science Majors

	4/C		3/C		2/C		1/C	
	Fall	Spring	Fall	Spring	Fall	Spring	Fall	Spring
C O R E	Leadership	Naval Science	Navigation	Ethics	Tactics	Leadership	Law for JO	JO Practicum
	Chemistry1	Chemistry2	Physics1	Physics2	EE1	EE2		
	Calculus1	Calculus2	Calculus3	Differential Equations		Free Elective	Wpns & Systems Eng	
	English1	English2	WestCiv1	WestCiv2				
	Naval Heritage	US Gov & Constitution			Humanities SocSci Elctv			Humanities SocSci Elctv
D I V							Naval Eng1	Naval Eng2
M A J O R			Major Course	Major Course	Major Course	Major Course	Major Course	Major Course
			Major Course	Major Course	Major Course	Major Course	Major Course	Major Course
					Major Course	Major Course	Major Course	Major Course

A generic course matrix for group II majors at the U.S. Naval Academy.
Courtesy of Fredrick Davis

The Division of Humanities and Social Sciences, comprised of five departments, offers four majors:

Economics   History
English   Political science

Those majoring in economics, English, history, or political science—group III or "bull majors"—must take or validate a minimum of four semesters (twelve credits) in Chinese, French, German, Japanese, Russian, or Spanish. (At the time of this printing, there was consideration of including Arabic to the list of languages.) Language courses are given by the division's department of language studies (the fifth department in the division), which offers minors in all six languages, but no majors. To earn a minor in a foreign language, a midshipman must have a 3.0 average in his or her language courses and complete eight to twelve credits in advanced-level courses.

Midshipmen in group III majors represent about 35 percent of the Academy's upperclass. The "Division of Humanities and Social Sciences Majors" chart outlines a generic course matrix for group III majors.

While the Academy strives to allow each midshipman to major in the subject desired, caps do exist on certain majors. These caps derive

Division of Humanities and Social Sciences Majors

	4/C Fall	4/C Spring	3/C Fall	3/C Spring	2/C Fall	2/C Spring	1/C Fall	1/C Spring
	Leadership	Naval Science	Navigation	Ethics	Tactics	Leadership	Law for JO	JO Practicum
C	Chemistry1	Chemistry2	Physics1	Physics2	EE1	EE2		
O R	Calculus1	Calculus2	Calculus3	Probability & Statistics		Free Elective	Wpns & Systems Eng	
E	English1	English2	WestCiv1	WestCiv2				
	Naval Heritage	US Gov & Constitution			Humanities SocSci Elctv			Humanities SocSci Elctv
D I V							Naval Eng1	Naval Eng2
			Language1	Language2	Language3	Language4		
M			Major Course	Major Course	Major Course	Major Course	Major Course	Major Course
A J					Major Course	Major Course	Major Course	Major Course
O R							Major Course	Major Course

A generic course matrix for group III majors at the U.S. Naval Academy.
Courtesy of Fredrick Davis

primarily from available faculty in particular departments. The vast majority of midshipmen, however, are able to major in their first-choice subject.

The Academy's fourth division, the Division of Professional Development, is partly academic and partly professional. Its primary mission is to properly prepare midshipmen to become Navy and Marine Corps officers. The division, frequently referred to as "ProDev," consists of two teaching departments: (1) leadership and law, and (2) seamanship and navigation. Additionally, ProDev has one nonacademic department: professional programs. The two academic departments offer core curriculum and elective courses while the professional programs department primarily schedules midshipmen summer training, career information briefs, and everything related to service assignment.

Honors and Graduate Programs

Six selected majors—mathematics, oceanography and all four group III majors (economics, English, history, and political science)—have honors programs. Midshipmen who complete such programs graduate with honors in that major. To qualify for graduation with honors in a major, a midshipman must have (1) a cumulative quality point rating (CQPR) of 3.0, (2) a CQPR of 3.5 in courses in the major, (c) a 2.5 CQPR in professional courses, and (d) no Ds or Fs on the final transcript.

The Trident scholar program allows selected midshipmen with particular academic strengths—and standing in the top 10 percent of their class—to take reduced course loads in their final year to accommodate research and the writing of a thesis under an adviser's guidance. The number of Trident scholars varies widely from year to year, ranging between three and fifteen.

The voluntary graduate education program (VGEP) allows up to twenty top academic performers who complete their Academy academic requirements by the end of the first semester of their first class year to enroll in graduate classes at any of seven area universities. Such midshipmen graduate with their class and receive their commissions. They then have the opportunity to earn their Master's degrees within seven months before they have to report to their first duty assignments.

Midshipmen also can choose from a variety of graduate programs and scholarships, including a medical or dental school program for up to fifteen graduates; the Burke program; Olmsted, FitzGerald, and Pownall scholarships; and direct graduate education and delayed graduate education programs. Visit www.usna.edu/GraduateEducation for more current and specific graduate education information. Many Navy and Marine Corps officers pursue graduate study at some time. Those taking advantage of programs funded by the government that last a year or more generally must commit to two or three years of additional duty for each year of graduate study. Like life, few things in the Navy come free of charge.

Grades

The Academy uses the same grading system many high schools and colleges in the United States use, but it can still get confusing. Teachers award letter grades—without pluses and minuses—but then numbers take over.

For purposes of calculating averages, every letter grade has a quality point equivalent (QPE):

A=4	C=2	F=0
B=3	D=1	

A midshipman computes his or her quality point ratio (QPR)—what high school students call a GPA—in the following manner. For each course, multiply the QPE by its credit value (usually the number of times the course meets per week). For example, if the midshipman has a C in calculus and calculus meets four times per week, then multiply 2 (a C equals 2 points) by 4 (for four hours per week). Add the resulting products for all courses taken. Divide that sum by the sum of the credit values for all courses taken. That number, rounded to two decimal places, is the QPR—generally expressed for six, twelve, and sixteen weeks as a semester quality point ratio (SQPR) or overall as a cumulative quality point ratio (CQPR). The latter is often called—phonetically—a see-kyooper. In cases of repeated courses in which the original course grade was a D or an F, the repeated course grade replaces the earlier grade in the CQPR. Summer school grades are similarly incorporated into the CQPR.

But that is not all. Although a GPA or CQPR is important, it is only 65 percent of the story. A midshipman's class standing, or order of merit, reflects not only academics but his or her grades in conduct, military performance, physical education, and athletics. Only when those grades are factored into an academic average does a midshipman arrive at his or her order of merit, on the basis of which certain privileges are dispensed.

Midshipmen performing especially well may make one of three lists.

Superintendent's List (made by about 6 percent of midshipmen): semester QPR of at least 3.4, with no semester grades below a C; an A in military performance; an A in conduct; at least a B in physical education. Qualifiers may wear a gold star on certain uniforms.

Dean's List (made by about 15 percent of midshipmen): those not on the Superintendent's List but those with a semester QPR of at least 3.4 and no failures in any course or professional area. Qualifiers may wear a bronze star on certain uniforms.

Commandant's List (made by about 22 percent of midshipmen): semester QPR of at least 2.9; at least a B in military performance; an A in conduct; at least a B in physical education. Qualifiers wear no special insignia, but may, as upperclass, be awarded extra liberty.

In addition, at graduation those in the top 10 percent of the order of merit ranking receive their degrees "with distinction." Those below the

President George W. Bush hands a very happy new graduate her diploma.
Courtesy of USNA

top 10 percent yet achieving 75 percent of the maximum order of merit score receive their degrees "with merit."

Grades are sent to parents each semester if the midshipman has authorized the Academy to do so. Without authorization, the Academy will not mail out grades and parents may never know how their midshipman is doing. This may be a midshipman's wish, and unsuspecting parents would never be the wiser. Parents who desire knowledge of their midshipman's grades should request such notification.

-3-

Military

For those unfamiliar with the Naval Academy, its military aspects rank high among its many mysteries. This aspect, more than any other, distinguishes the Academy from civilian colleges. The military aspect makes life at the Academy nearly unique. Today's Naval Academy graduates only account for about one-third of all new naval officers; collegiate Naval Reserve Officer Training Corps

The color guard and nearby midshipmen stand perfectly still as a mist falls over the parade ground.
Courtesy of USNA

(NROTC) programs produce about one-third and officer candidate school (OCS) about one-third. The U.S. Naval Academy, however, is fundamentally the U.S. Navy's college. Not surprisingly, the military side of the school is dominant—even controlling.

The Academy's near-synonym for *military* is *professional,* but the two words connote slight differences. *Military* is the broader word, meaning the noncivilian regimen; *professional* is narrower, suggesting the squaring away of midshipmen in terms of military bearing, performance, attitude, and knowledge of the naval profession. Military/professional training begins on Induction Day (see I-Day discussion below and in chapter 8) and lasts throughout one's stay at the Academy. The Division of Professional Development (ProDev) is one of the Academy's most notable, and influential, aspects. By and large, it oversees the more than two thousand hours (including approximately forty-five semester hours in class) of military/professional training each midshipman receives.

Officers and upperclass continuously evaluate a midshipman's professional (military) aptitude, for example, on inspections, on attitude and bearing, on leadership potential, and on general behavior. The resulting performance grades, known as "aptitude for commission," constitute about 25 percent of a midshipman's class rank (or order of merit). Those not measuring up may find themselves on the road home.

Bancroft Hall

Although drill does exist as a dreary and loathsome (by the mids) constant, the crucible for the professional military training is not the parade field. Most training occurs in Bancroft Hall.

Main entrance of Bancroft Hall through Tecumseh Court.
Courtesy of USNA

Midshipmen call Bancroft Hall either "Bancroft" or "the Hall." It is where practically everything happens. Bancroft is the vast dormitory housing all midshipmen—no exceptions. Midshipmen dwell in rooms there. They eat in a part of it: King Hall. They are reminded of naval and Marine Corps traditions by another part of it: the quasi-sacred Memorial Hall.

Midshipmen study at Bancroft, are inspected there, and are trained and disciplined there. They do pranks there, although not nearly as many nowadays as was done only a few years ago. They do chow calls there. They form up there during cold or inclement weather. In the Hall's basement they buy books and uniforms and do other shopping at the Midshipmen Store (Midstore). In the basement, they also can get their hair cut and shaped, take their uniforms for tailoring or cleaning and their shoes for resoling, get their cavities filled and their broken arms set, and pick up packages and mail their letters (when they write).

Bancroft probably is the world's largest dormitory. Its current value is listed at $1.2 billion. In 2003 it completed an eleven-year, $251 million renovation. It has eight wings, containing 1,646 rooms. There are nearly five miles of hallway on the five floors and two basement levels. It has 1.4 million square feet of floor space. The budget for operating and maintaining Bancroft is estimated at $3 million per year.

Because Bancroft is a principal training area for individuals who one day will experience shipboard life, it carries ship (gray-hull) nomenclature. Its floors are *decks,* its walls *bulkheads,* its ceilings *overheads;* its stairways *ladders,* its hallways *passageways,* its drinking fountains *scuttlebutts.* Midshipmen stand watch there. Plebes wishing to enter an upperclass's room, as well as midshipmen wishing to enter an officer's office, must "request permission to come aboard."

Bancroft's fifty-five-thousand-square-foot dining area—or wardroom—is T-shaped King Hall. Twelve thousand hot meals are prepared there daily. In one hour the kitchen can fry a ton of shrimp or broil 3,000 hamburgers. It can simultaneously cook 750 gallons of soup or 320 turkeys weighing 12 to 16 pounds. In a typical day, it might serve 1,000 gallons of milk, a ton of green vegetables, two tons of meat and another two tons of potatoes, 720 pies, 1,200 loaves of bread, and 300 gallons of ice cream. King Hall has 372 tables. Peanut butter and jelly, along with an assortment of condiments, is available at each table. Most midshipmen eat with their squad at "squad tables," although in-season varsity athletes eat the same meal as everyone else with their teammates at "team tables." Breakfast and lunch are served by King Hall staff. Dinner is buffet style, except for Wednesday nights when no one has liberty.

Midshipmen eat in King Hall.
Courtesy of USNA

Classes

The Naval Academy does not use conventional collegiate names for its class members. Instead, the following terms are used:

Freshman: fourth class (called a plebe)
Sophomore: third class (called a youngster)
Junior: second class (called a second class)
Senior: .   first class (called a firstie or first class)

Each class has specific military duties. Plebes make the transition from civilian or high-school life. They learn about the U.S. Navy and U.S. Marine Corps, and how to perform under pressure. Youngsters help the second class train the plebes and supplement their knowledge. Second class train the plebes. First class duties include overseeing plebe training, running the company, and assisting commanding officers in running the Brigade.

During Plebe Summer, plebes march everywhere. Detailers are on the right.
Courtesy of USNA

Plebes

As the last in—the newest boys and girls on the block—plebes stand at the bottom of the heap. Having been for the most part outstanding in high school, they enter the Naval Academy and are immediately reduced to insignificance and near-nothingness. Certain "rights" are withdrawn; these rights are now considered privileges that midshipmen earn later.

Plebes are permitted almost no property. Essentially they are allowed basic necessities, including toilet articles, a watch, an alarm clock, and a calculator. Other items allowed may include snapshots, a small lamp, a small fan, special athletic equipment (such as lacrosse sticks or tennis racquets), a book or two, and limited clothing. Items n⸢ ⸣
I-Day must be carried. They are stored thereafter, and may c⸢ ⸣
grief than they are worth. Inductees may prefer that these ite⸢ ⸣
later when the new midshipman asks for them.

Plebes are accorded practically no privileges and certainly no prestige (save that in the eyes of their parents and high school mates). From the moment they are shorn on I-Day, plebes' egos suffer systematic indignities. They deal with a lot of "don'ts," notably the prohibitions against the possession of cars or anything electronic or battery-operated that emits sound.

Plebe Summer, which consists primarily of physical training and military indoctrination, is tough. So is plebe year—particularly the portion called the Dark Ages, following Christmas vacation. Candidates (or appointees) technically become plebes and members of the fourth class on Induction Day. At the annual Herndon (Plebe Recognition Ceremony) in May they finally shed the stigma of being a plebe. They remain members of the fourth class only until graduation several days later, when they become members of the third class. According to the tradition stated in *Reef Points*, the plebe manual, third class do not become youngsters until they see the chapel dome upon returning from their youngster cruise.

Midshipmen work together to climb Herndon.
Courtesy of Andrea Mackenzie

Brigade Organization

All midshipmen constitute the Brigade of Midshipmen. The Brigade is divided into a number of constituent parts, and largely as a result of Bancroft Hall renovations, those constituent parts have varied over the last decade. The principle variation stemmed from the difference in the overall number of companies: thirty or thirty-six. Currently the Brigade has thirty companies, but the administration's hope is to increase that size back to thirty-six in coming years. Regardless, the organization remains the same. The Brigade is equally divided into two regiments. Each regiment is equally divided into three battalions. Each battalion is equally divided into companies. Each company consists of four platoons. Each platoon consists of three squads. After Plebe Summer each midshipmen receives his or her assignment. For example, one mid might be assigned to First Regiment, Third Battalion, Ninth Company, Second Platoon, Third Squad and another mid would be assigned to Second Regiment, Fourth Battalion, Twentieth Company, First Platoon, First Squad. Numbers vary due to attrition, but each squad, the most basic unit, generally has twelve midshipmen—one or two who are first class, and three or four from each of the other classes.

The major administrative unit in the Brigade is the company. Each company generally has about 140 midshipmen, approximately 35 from each class. Each company has a commissioned Company Officer, a senior enlisted adviser (SEL), and a company commander (a firstie). Except for out-of-company mega-stripers, midshipmen may room only in a "company area" with other members of their company and class. The method of scrambling plebes into other companies frequently changes. (See *shuffling* and *shotgunning* entries in the Midspeak dictionary [Chapter 8].)

Rank and Insignia

All midshipmen wear insignia on their uniforms that designate their class or—within the first class—their rank (see table 4). All classes wear ribbons, medals, or warfare specialty insignia (the last either from prior enlistment or from summer training) over their left breast pocket. Those entitled to a Superintendent's List gold star, a Dean's List bronze star, or to a varsity letter "N" wear them on the flap of the left breast pocket. The Superintendent's stars are also worn above the anchors that midshipmen wear on lapels of their SDBs (service dress blues) or on the collars of their service dress whites. Those in the color company or in the drum and bugle corps wear, respectively, an "E" or a bugle.

Table 4. Midshipmen Uniform Insignia Designating Class and Rank

Class	Sleeve	Shoulder Board	Collar
Plebes	no insignia	Anchor with stripes corresponding to their sleeves[1]	no insignia
Youngsters	One slanted gold stripe on left sleeve		anchor on right collar only
Second Class	Two slanted gold stripes on left sleeves		anchor on left and right collar
First Class	One horizontal stripe on both sleeves		eagle on left and right collar[2]

[1]For a picture illustrating the midshipmen shoulder boards and rank, visit www.usna-net.org/handbook/summer.html#boards.

[2]Upperclass also wear collar insignia—but no sleeve or shoulder insignia—on their raincoats and their blue working jackets.

Stripers

Within the Brigade, primarily within the first class, certain midshipmen (about one-tenth of the firsties) hold one-semester rank corresponding to their duties in the Brigade or their regiment, battalion, platoon, company, or squad.

First class midshipmen who have no specific duties during a particular semester are referred to as midshipmen-in-ranks (MIRs). They wear one horizontal stripe with an anchor on each shoulder board. The remaining firsties are considered stripers and wear one star and one horizontal stripe on their sleeves and shoulder boards; they are called midshipman ensigns. All firsties wear one star; stripes designate rank:

Two stripes:	midshipman lieutenant junior grade
Three stripes:	midshipman lieutenant
Four stripes:	midshipman lieutenant commander
Five stripes:	midshipman commander
Six stripes:	midshipman captain

These boards are nicely displayed at www.usna-net.org/handbook/summer.html#boards.

The Brigade commander—the highest-ranking midshipman—crosses her hands over the hilt of her sword.
Courtesy of USNA

The Brigade commander, who wears six stripes, is the top-ranking midshipman. He or she is assisted by regimental commanders and other stripers. Stripers are selected through a complex process based on interviews, evaluations, and Academy records. Striper billets, or positions, are for one semester only. Usually no firsties except Brigade commanders will wear a combined total of more than six stripes during the year.

In addition, as an extension of the chain of command, there are nonfirstie stripers—second class who assist firsties with the administration of their companies and the Brigade. They wear no special insignia designating their rank, but are called Brigade or regimental sergeant majors and company first sergeants.

Uniforms

Uniform regulations and restrictions specific to the Naval Academy are one of the many things that usually change with each new Commandant of Midshipmen and/or Superintendent. The information given below is intended as a guide only. Current regulations must be followed by all midshipmen.

Uniforms occupy a major place in a midshipman's life, and beyond. Midshipmen generally rotate into and out of seasonal uniforms when other Navy personnel do. For the most part, midshipman uniforms correspond to those worn Navy-wide: white in warm and hot weather, black in cool and cold. (Note: what the Navy considers and refers to as "blue" is actually black to the rest of the world.)

During Plebe Summer, plebes wear whiteworks—the closest thing the Academy has to a white "Cracker Jack" sailor suit. At the Academy in the summer, upperclass wear either summer whites or short-sleeved summer khakis.

During the academic year, midshipmen on the Yard wear their working uniforms: summer working blues (short-sleeved), or winter working blues (long-sleeved). At night or outside the Yard, midshipmen must wear summer whites or service dress blues (SDBs). For more formal occasions, they wear either (1) full dress whites (choker whites) during the day, (2) dinner dress whites and dinner dress blues at night, or (3) full dress whites or full dress blues (chokers).

For those interested in wading through hundreds of pages detailing the U.S. Navy's uniform regulations, visit https://buperscd.technology. navy.mil/bup_updt/508/unireg/uregMenu.html. For specific information and photographs (some of which are quite dated) of all Navy uniforms, visit https://buperscd.technology.navy.mil/bup_updt/upd_ CD/BUPERS/ Unireg/Chapter3.PDF.

There are many different types of uniforms that midshipmen wear. They have a seemingly limitless collection of uniform clothing and paraphernalia, including infantry dress, dungarees, camouflage fatigues, and PE (physical education) gear. They also have a three-button reefer (similar to a Navy pea-coat), a four-button overcoat, and a loose-fitting, lightweight jacket referred to as an "Ike" jacket because it was the preferred jacket of former president Dwight D. Eisenhower. They have a monogrammed blue and gold jogging suit. Finally, the midshipmen possess various types of shoes, for example, leathers (white and black), corfams, shower shoes, and sneakers.

All midshipmen must wear uniforms at all times except when they are at their sponsor's house or with their parents in private, or when on an authorized weekend or leave. Firsties and second class on such a weekend or leave may wear civilian clothes when entering or leaving the Yard. Midshipmen may wear only their N sweater with civilian clothes. In

Midshipmen line up in choker whites for a special drill ceremony.
Courtesy of USNA

place of a coat and without a cover, they may also wear N sweaters with summer or winter working blue uniforms and with SDBs.

Honor

The Academy can be a stressful, taxing environment. Inappropriate behavior can and does occur.

Honor offenses—primarily lying, cheating, and stealing—may result in dismissal, which is called separation. I say *may* because much has changed in recent years regarding the handling of honor offenses. In 1986 the U.S. Naval Academy changed the long-standing honor concept. Before then, it read, quite simply, "Midshipmen do not lie, cheat or steal." Because this sounded "too negative," a modified concept took its place. Between 1986 and 1993 the honor concept read, "Midshipmen are persons of integrity: They do not lie, cheat, or steal." Then, as a result of the 1992 electrical engineering cheating scandal by USNA's class of 1994, the Academy began to seriously investigate the honor concept and the ways in which honor offenses were handled. In fact, an entire new division—the Character Development Division—was created to handle honor-related issues and honor "education." In the process, the Academy's honor code was again updated. Today, it reads,

Midshipmen are persons of integrity: They stand for that which is right. They tell the truth and ensure that the full truth is known. They do not lie. They embrace fairness in all actions. They ensure that work submitted as their own is their own, and that assistance received from any source is authorized and properly documented. They do not cheat. They respect the property of others and ensure that others are able to benefit from the use of their own property. They do not steal.

After the changes in the wording of the honor concept, the Academy began to consider the severity of guilty findings in particular honor cases. It determined that even guilty parties could—and, indeed, should in some cases—be retained. The Academy determined that these midshipmen could be "remediated" by regularly meeting with a "moral remediator," a faculty member who would discuss moral, ethical, and honor issues with the midshipman. This mentor's label has changed; today such individuals are called "honor remediators."

Honor is taken very seriously by the Academy, and the process by which midshipmen are accused and tried is extremely complex. It, however, like all systems, has flaws. From interviews conducted I learned that flaws include those perceived by midshipmen as well as faculty and administrators.

In cases of alleged honor offenses, the Brigade honor committee comes into play. The Brigade-wide committee consists of midshipmen-elected honor stripers who serve year-round. Some are elected at the Brigade level, some at the battalion level, and some at the company level. The committee's chairman reviews each case and determines whether to counsel the individual or to refer the case to an honor board consisting of members of the committee. If an honor board finds the allegations in a given case likely to be true, the honor committee refers the case to the Commandant. If the case results in a recommendation from the Commandant for separation, it then goes to the Superintendent and then—for final disposition—to the Secretary of the Navy.

For more information about the Character Development Division, visit www.usna.edu/CharacterDevelopment/homepage.html. For more information about the honor aspect of the Character Development Division, visit www.usna.edu/CharacterDevelopment/honor/honor_index.html.

Conduct

Midshipman conduct is a massive issue. Conduct offenses result in disciplinary measures (restriction, extra duty, extra military instruction, and tours). Serious offenses (like an honor offense) may also result in separation.

All midshipmen are given both conduct and performance grades (A–F), both of which are ultimately reflected in order of merit rankings. Conduct grades are based on the number of demerits a midshipman has received. Performance grades have recently been changed to the "aptitude for commission" grade. The system now incorporates the "whole-person" concept and includes conduct, teacher/instructor evaluations, evals/FITREPS, and a newly developed peer ranking system in which peers (classmates) in the same company rank each other between 1 and 30-something (however many there are) and upperclass rank all underclass. Company Officers rank everybody. These numbers get calculated and a grade is determined. The Company Officer, however, retains ultimate authority regarding performance grades.

A midshipman accused of a conduct infraction is "fried." To be fried means—in civilian terms—to be charged, indicted, or put on report. Upon investigation, the "fry" may be dropped or its disposition may be some form of punishment. There used to exist pieces of paper called "Form 2s" which were akin to a demerit slip. Form 2s have been abandoned thanks to the advent of computers. Now, all frys are "e-frys"; notification of a conduct infraction arrives via e-mail.

Alleged conduct offenses are dealt with administratively, in a nonjudicial fashion, as they are elsewhere in the fleet. Conduct expectations are outlined in the eighty-seven page *Midshipmen Regulations*, called Mid Regs for short. *Midshipmen Regulations* discusses almost everything midshipmen need to know to stay out of trouble. It covers everything from schedules to liberty, dating, drinking, how to arrange and inspect rooms, Navy customs, pay and finances, and much more.

There is also an administrative conduct system that spells out various dos and don'ts. The conduct system separates infractions into two main categories: major offenses (majors), and minor offenses (minors). All major level infractions are potentially separation-level offenses. The decision to separate or not is based on the nature of the infraction, the history of the midshipman in question, and the reports from the midshipman's chain of command. Examples of major infractions are:

Violation of orders
Aggravated violation of mid regs
Intentional failure to perform a duty
Violation of honor concept
Violation or abuse of the training system
Hazing
Sexual harassment
Sexual misconduct
Fraternization
Disrespect/insubordination
Drinking in violation of local, state, and/or federal law(s)
Drinking on duty
Trafficking alcohol in Bancroft Hall
Possession, use, or selling of illicit drugs (including marijuana, ecstasy, and anabolic steroids)
Absent without authority (UA):
   Greater than 30 minutes
   Less than 24 hours
   Greater than 24 hours

Major infractions are adjudicated by the Commandant. The Commandant, however, often delegates the duty to the Deputy Commandant or Battalion Officers. Minor infractions include:

Violation of mid regs
Failure to know plebe rates
Improper conduct in ranks
Unauthorized wearing of class insignia or rank
Wearing civilian clothes when not authorized
Unprepared for inspection
Negligent or careless destruction of government property
UA less then 15 minutes
UA from military obligation
UA from academic class
Usurping privileges
Failure to perform duty

The U.S. Naval Academy's rotunda is located just inside the main entrance of Bancroft Hall. Memorial Hall can be seen in the distance.

Courtesy of USNA

Minor infractions are adjudicated by the Company Officer. The Company Officer often delegates the duty to the midshipman company commander.

Punishments, of course, vary depending on the severity of an infraction. Thankfully for the midshipmen, there do exist limits to punishments. Obviously the maximum punishment would be separation. Short of that, table 5 shows the punishment limits for majors and minors.

All conduct infractions—majors and minors—remain on a midshipman's record until graduation.

One final note about conduct concerns the "Black N." Midshipmen who manage to get into a heap of trouble have the possibility of earning a Black N. Black Ns are not sanctioned by the Academy administration. In fact, their mere presence and existence is significantly frowned upon

Table 5. Maximum Allowable Punishment for Major and Minor Conduct Infractions

Punishment	Majors	Minors
Demerits	100	35
Restriction[1]	60 days	None
Tours[2]	20	2 possible for every 5 demerits
EMI[3] (hours)	30	15
Loss of privileges	Up to 1 year	Up to 1 month
Loss of leave	Up to 1 year	Does not apply
Conduct probation	Up to 1 year	Does not apply

[1]Restriction is a nice way of saying "minimum security prison." Midshipmen on restriction work off demerits over a period of days while they are literally restricted to the confines of the Yard. They may not—under any circumstances—leave the Academy grounds. Additionally, they may not leave their company area except for (1) classes, (2) athletics, and (3) restriction musters. Throughout the day, even regular academic days, "restrictees" (those midshipmen on restriction) must report to a specified location to be inspected by the officer of the watch, one of the Academy's senior watchstanders. During a regular school day, there are usually two musters: one before classes and one in the evening. During the weekends there may be as many as five or six musters, with some of them being "surprise" musters intended to catch unsuspecting restrictees off-guard. Should a period of restriction extend into or through a leave period or vacation, upperclass will remain at the Academy during that period.

[2]Tours are marched with a rifle, either outside Bancroft or inside near the battalion office, and occasionally in other areas. A tour is usually forty-five minutes. Sometimes a midshipman may be given a "room tour" in which he or she serves the tour in his or her room studying.

[3]EMI is the acronym for extra military instruction. It involves instruction commensurate with the conduct infraction. For example, a midshipman fried for poor uniform appearance may be asked to practice getting into an inspection-ready uniform and subsequently get inspected, over and over and over.

because administration officials believe it is wrong to celebrate those who break the rules. That said, however, Black Ns are very real. The physical award for a Black N is a sweater whose colors are almost the photo negative of the varsity athlete N sweater; a Black N sweater is bright yellow with (logically) a Black N sewn on it. Specific rules for earning Black Ns do exist but are not public. Simply said, a midshipman must be very close to separation yet be retained to be eligible to earn a Black N. Those who tempt fate more than once, by again getting into a heap of trouble and again getting retained, may earn a black star to sew on their sweater in the same way that athletes earn a star for victories over an Army team. The only time these sweaters may be worn by their owners is during the annual Halloween costume dinner. Tradition has it that those who have Black Ns line up and parade through King Hall during dinner, usually to a standing ovation by the rest of the Brigade and the scowls of the administration.

Separation

Separation is the term used for someone who leaves the Academy. It takes one of two basic forms: voluntary resignation or involuntary discharge.

If voluntary, a midshipman usually separates because of unhappiness or incompatibility; the Naval Academy experience has proved to be something other than what the individual had expected. A midshipman also might voluntarily resign if he or she faces the prospect of dismissal for reasons of academics or discipline; this is known as a "qualified resignation."

Midshipmen who separate in their plebe or youngster year face no subsequent obligation of military service (unless they had prior enlistments that have not been completed to date). They may, however, be asked to reimburse the Academy for the value of their education thus far and will be asked to pay off all expenses and loans.

Midshipmen who separate after the beginning of classes for their second class year will be asked to reimburse the Academy for education costs to date and/or to serve as enlisted sailors in the fleet for a period of time. The length of service required is longer for those who separate later in their Academy experience.

Each separation is dealt with on an individual basis with different outcomes depending on each particular set of circumstances. The following are the Academy's general rules regarding separations. A USNA reimbursement calculation is based on supplies, room, board, teachers' salaries, and so on. It can prove to be a large number, running in excess of $250,000 for all four years of school. The United States Code (federal law) governs the separation process. The Secretary of the Navy must personally approve all Academy separations, whether voluntary or involuntary for academics or discipline.

Summer Training

Midshipmen participate in summer training to learn more about the U.S. Navy and the U.S. Marine Corps and to learn about future career options. Summer training begins with Plebe Summer. After induction (usually the last week of June or the first week of July), plebes endure their first training until Parents Weekend in August.

Thereafter, summer training consists of two out of three one-month "blocks" every summer. Upperclass thus usually serve eight out of twelve weeks. Some cruises, primarily for rising youngsters, however, are only three weeks. This complicates things, because the summer is then comprised of four three-week blocks. Yet eight weeks of required training for

Plebes work together (during Plebe Summer) in an inflatable Zodiac boat.
Courtesy of USNA

each class is comprised of one mandatory block and one elective block. Depending on class standing, on what is requested, and on the vagaries of scheduling, midshipman might serve the first two blocks, the last two, or the first and last. The block in which they do not do summer training is available for summer leave unless another elective training block is chosen.

The USNA summer training department—part of the Division of Professional Development—performs an extraordinary task each summer. They try to accommodate each midshipman's desires and routinely schedule over sixty-two hundred assignments (two blocks for over three thousand midshipmen) in locations literally all over the world. The schedulers wade through the logistical quagmire every summer. Knowing this, each midshipman may better understand the impossibility of accommodating each individual's wish.

Summer training is another aspect of the Academy that changes frequently with new administrations. While writing this book, midshipmen summer training was in the midst of a major overhaul that was complicated by the fact that our country was at war. For obvious reasons, the available platforms on which midshipmen may train was limited. While training specifics and global situations change, the general goals of the summer training department are outlined in table 6. The classes referred to indicate the year a midshipman will be in the upcoming fall; for example, "youngster" refers to a rising youngster (those who have just completed plebe year).

Liberty and Leave

Leave is the term used for the longer amounts of time off. It includes summer, Thanksgiving, Christmas, and spring vacations. Liberty is the term used for short amounts of time off, usually no more than ninety-six hours (four days). It comes in three basic forms: Yard liberty, town liberty, and weekend liberty. The specifics of USNA liberty and leave, like so many other things, frequently change with new administrations. The information provided below is intended as guidelines only.

Yard liberty is the freedom to go most places on the Academy campus. Generally, all midshipmen have Yard liberty daily from 5:30 AM until taps. Midshipmen must wear the uniform of the day during Yard liberty unless they are participating in athletic events.

Town liberty is the freedom to visit Annapolis and its immediate environs, within a twenty-two-mile limit. For a map of this limit, visit www.usna-net.org/handbook/22mile.html. Midshipmen must wear the

Table 6. USNA Summer Program Choices by Class

Youngster

Mandatory Cruise Block	Elective Training Block
LANTPAT (YP cruise)	Command seamanship and navigation training squadron (CSNTS)
	Navy tactical training (NTT)
	Summer Seminar
	SCUBA school (Panama City, Florida)
	Varsity offshore sailing team (VOST)

Second class

Mandatory Cruise Block	Elective Training Block
Surface cruise	Professional training for midshipmen (PROTRAMID)
Submarine cruise	Plebe/weapons/NAPS detail
	Airborne school
	VOST
	Language study abroad program (LSAP)

First class

Mandatory Cruise Block	Elective Training Block
Surface cruise	CSNTS
Submarine cruise	Plebe/weapons/NAPS detail
Aviation cruise	Second Fleet cruise
Leatherneck (USMC)	MAGTF cruise (USMC)
Explosive ordinance disposal (EOD) cruise	Summer seminar
Mini-BUD/S (SEALs)	LANTPAT (YP cruise)
Foreign exchange cruise	Approved internship
French training cruise	VOST
	SCUBA school
	Airborne school

uniform of the day during town liberty. Town liberty does not extend overnight.

Firsties have liberty each weekday from 4:00 PM (or following their last military obligation, whichever is later) until 10:00 PM (except Wednesdays). On Saturday firsties have liberty from the morning liberty formation until 1:00 AM; on Sunday they have it until 8:00 PM.

Second class and youngsters have liberty on Saturday and Sunday at the same times as the firsties. Plebes have liberty on Saturday until 10:00 PM. Otherwise, plebes have no town liberty.

Weekend liberty is for midshipmen who are not deficient in academics, physical education, conduct, or performance. Firsties have an unlimited number of weekends, consistent with their obligations. Second class have six weekends of liberty per semester. Youngsters have three per semester. Plebes have no weekend liberty unless authorized. Midshipmen with particularly strong academic and military performance, notably those on the Superintendent's List and Dean's Lists, may (under some administrations) receive additional weekend liberty.

–4–

Athletics and Physical Education

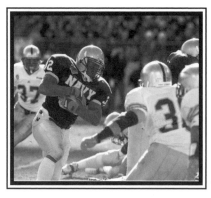

A Navy player guards the ball as he runs through Army's line.
Courtesy of USNA

The Naval Academy requires four years of physical education and year-round athletics. Every midshipman must participate in a sport—intercollegiate, intramural, or club. Usually, those on varsity or junior varsity (JV) squads participate in or train for their sport year round. Therefore, they are exempt from having to compete at intramural or club levels in what civilian colleges might consider off-seasons.

For example, varsity and JV midshipmen do not ordinarily play intramural or club sports. They usually do not play on more than one varsity-level team. Midshipmen on varsity and JV teams also are exempt from some marching and parade drill, an ongoing battle that rages between Academy coaches and Bancroft Hall administration. Under the National Collegiate Athletic Association (NCAA) guidelines, coaches may only conduct team practices for twenty hours per week.

Intercollegiate Athletics

The Academy offers competition in numerous intercollegiate varsity and junior-varsity sports for both men and women. (See table 7.)

Table 7. Intercollegiate Sports at the U.S. Naval Academy

Intercollegiate Varsity Sports

Men	Women
Baseball	Basketball
Basketball	Crew
Crew (heavyweight)	Cross country
Crew (lightweight)	Sailing
Cross country	Soccer
Football	Swimming
Sprint football (150-pound)	Track (indoor)
Golf	Track (outdoor)
Gymnastics	Volleyball
Lacrosse	
Rifle	
Sailing (intercollegiate and offshore)	
Soccer	
Squash	
Swimming	
Tennis	
Track (indoor)	
Track (outdoor)	
Water polo	
Wrestling	

Intercollegiate Junior Varsity Sports

Men	Women
Baseball	Basketball
Basketball	Crew
Crew (heavyweight)	
Crew (lightweight)	
Football	
Golf	
Rifle	
Squash	
Tennis	
Wrestling	

A Navy basketball play-
er goes for a lay-up.
Courtesy of USNA

Because JV squads are considered feeders for varsity squads, mid-shipmen almost never compete on JV squads beyond youngster year. If they do not make varsity teams by their second class year, they usually move to intramural or club competition. Additionally, the Academy offers interscholastic competition for plebes in crew for both men and women. A wealth of information is available online. The two primary resourses for Navy intercollegiate sports information are www.usna.edu/athletics.htm and www.navysports.com/.

Intramural Athletics

Intramural sports cover a broad range. Some are played at the company level, while others are played at the battalion level. When their members do not have military obligations, intramural teams practice three after-noons per week for two hours each. Contrary to members of in-season varsity and JV teams, members of intramural teams have no marching or parade drill exemptions. Coaches, managers, and referees are usually first class or second class midshipmen. Intramurals are coed.

The fall intramural sports are flag football, soccer, basketball (5 on 5), tennis, batallion sailboating, and cross country. The winter sports are batallion basketball (3 on 3), boxing, fieldball, flickerball, racquetball, and street hockey. The spring sports are wrestling, half marathon, disc football, softball, 6-a-side soccer, and team handball.

Club Sports

Club sports differ somewhat from intramurals. They begin as extracurricular activities (ECAs) and must remain ECAs for four years, at which time they may be elevated to club status. Currently several sports are ECAs, and could become certified club sports. Like intramural teams, club teams practice for about two hours on three afternoons each week if their members do not have military obligations. Club members are not drill exempt. As every intercollegiate team does, each club team must have an O-Rep (discussed below). Such teams arrange their own schedules and travel. They compete against similar teams at collegiate or postcollegiate levels.

Club sports for men are boxing, ice hockey, lacrosse, rugby, and volleyball. Club sports for women are gymnastics, lacrosse, tennis, rugby, and softball. Co-ed club sports are combat pistol, cycle, judo, karate, pistols, powerlifting, and triathalon. For more information about USNA's club sports, visit www.usna.edu/athletics.htm or www.usna.edu/PEScheds/clubhome.htm.

Leagues and Conferences

The Naval Academy is a member of the National Collegiate Athletic Association (NCAA), the Eastern Collegiate Athletic Conference (ECAC), the Eastern Intercollegiate Conference (EIC) for many respective sports, the Eastern Association of Rowing Colleges (EARC), and the Patriot League. Men's teams that compete in the Patriot League are baseball, basketball, golf, soccer, tennis, indoor track, and outdoor track; women's teams are basketball, cross country, soccer, swimming, indoor track, outdoor track, and volleyball. And—perhaps most important for midshipmen—Navy competes against Army in both intercollegiate and club competition twenty-one times per year.

Navy cheerleaders
exhibit their skills.
Courtesy of USNA

Athletic Association

The non-profit Naval Academy Athletic Association (NAAA, referred to as "N-triple-A") administers, promotes, and helps finance the Academy's intercollegiate athletic programs. Ticket sales (primarily football and men's basketball) and private contributions are the NAAA's primary sources of money. It hires coaches and staffs for such sports as football and men's basketball. It provides equipment, arranges for travel and lodging, sets schedules, sells tickets, and handles contest details. In accordance with NCAA guidelines, it also recruits. It operates and maintains the football stadium. NAAA runs the Naval Academy's Armel-Leftwich Visitors Center and the tour guide service, whose earnings help fund special events and various Brigade activities. In addition, NAAA assesses each midshipman about fifty dollars annually as an athletic activities fee for equipment, travel, and so on. This fee is in addition to each midshipman paying for his or her seat at each home football game. Attendance at each home football game is mandatory.

Facilities

The Academy's major athletic facilities include:

Navy–Marine Corps Memorial Stadium with seating for 30,000
Alumni Hall with seating for 5,700
6,217-yard golf course
Olympic-size swimming pool with seating for 1,000 in Lejeune Hall, plus a diving well
Water polo pool in Macdonough Hall
Lap tank pool in Macdonough Hall
Max Bishop baseball stadium with seating for 5,000
Synthetic-surfaced field for football, soccer, and lacrosse
400-meter all-weather outdoor track
220-yard indoor track
Dahlgren indoor ice hockey rink
50-foot-high rock climbing wall in Halsey Field House, hosting thirty graded climbs ranging from 5.4 to 5.11 on the Yosemite Decimal System (YDS), and numerous bouldering routes ranging from V0 to V8 on the Vermin scale

There is also a wrestling room, weight-training and personal conditioning rooms, gymnastics areas, boxing rings, shooting ranges, seventy-five acres of lighted fields, ten basketball courts, approximately fifty rowing shells, thirty tennis courts, and fifteen squash courts. For more information on the Academy sports facilities, visit www.usna.edu/athletics.htm.

Sailing

In conjunction with NAAA, the Naval Academy Sailing Squadron—housed with the sailing department and the Naval Academy Sailing Foundation in the Robert Crown Sailing Center—oversees the Academy's competitive sailing program. The Academy's resources afloat include about 250 craft—from 108-foot YPs (yard patrol crafts) to sloops to beautiful donated racing craft to Lasers, Colgates, and sailboards.

Members of Navy's offshore sailing team keel their boat over to gain an advantage over their opponents.
Courtesy of USNA

Officer Representatives and Faculty Representatives

Midshipmen on varsity, JV, plebe, and club teams have Officer Representatives, called "O-Reps"; some have Faculty Representatives, called "Fac Reps."

O-Reps, who are active-duty officers, must be approved annually. Technically, they work in the post for the Commandant and for the athletic director. They serve both as role models for team members and as links between the teams and the administration. They assist with finances for the teams, help arrange team transportation, and accompany the teams on away engagements. Sometimes O-Reps also serve as volunteer coaches, allowing for more flexibility on the part of the paid coach.

Fac Reps are full-time members of the Academy faculty and some are active-duty officers. They track the academic performance of team members and assist as necessary with such things as academic course scheduling and scheduling extra instruction. Sometimes Fac Reps travel with their respective team.

Team Tables

Athletes on in-season teams, or on teams with year-round commitments, frequently eat with their teammates at team tables (as opposed to the regular squad tables) in King Hall. In accordance with NCAA rules, athletes at such tables receive no special food.

Letters

Varsity letters, or Ns, are awarded to athletes for meeting specific criteria while participating in intercollegiate sports. In addition to the N, an individual is awarded a star that is worn with the letter when the individual's team defeats Army in the annual N-star competition. Approximately 460 men and 140 women win varsity letters each academic year. Varsity team managers can earn varsity letters and the accompanying star by meeting certain criteria. Other individuals who participate on an intercollegiate sports team for the entire competitive season but did not qualify for a letter are sometimes awarded the team N designation.

Physical Training

Every midshipman receives instruction in certain sports. In addition, every semester each midshipman must satisfy certain physical education (PE) requirements. All plebes receive instruction and grades in swimming and personal conditioning. All youngsters receive instruction and grades in swimming, boxing, and/or wrestling. All second class receive instruction and grades in swimming, judo, and one PE elective. All firsties receive instruction and grades in two PE electives.

The current electives from which all midshipmen may choose are:

Advanced rock climbing
Adventure challenge
Badminton
Basketball
Boxing aerobics
First aid
Golf

Gymnastics
Tennis
Hand-to-hand combat
Introduction to rock climbing
Kayaking
Lacrosse
Racquetball
Soccer
Softball
Squash
Swimming conditioning
Volleyball
Water polo
Weight training

A midshipman performs a curl-up during the biannual physical readiness test (PRT).
Courtesy of USNA

In addition to semester swimming tests, each midshipman must pass a physical readiness test (PRT) each semester. The PRT consists of a one and a half mile run or a five-hundred-yard swim, sit-ups, push-ups, and a sit and reach flexibility test. Different standards apply to each gender, further subdivided into age groups, the matrix for those standards is dizzying. In short, better performance earns better grades. One good perk goes to those mids who max out the PRT in the fall semester: they are excused from taking the PRT in the spring. On the other end of the spectrum, those failing the PRT lose some of their midshipman privileges. Midshipmen not meeting the requirements in any PE capacity (that is, those judged "PE deficient") are placed in the PE department remedial program. Those failing repeatedly likely will be put on probation or sent to the Academic Board for further review.

$-5-$

Money

Midshipmen await their turn at a Navy Federal Credit Union automatic teller machine (ATM) on the Yard.

Author photo

According to the federal government's General Accounting Office, the cost per graduate for the class of 2002 was $266,230. The figure is generated by taking the total amount of money it takes to run the Naval Academy and dividing it by the number of active midshipmen. A point of interest is that this figure is significantly less than the other two primary service academies (the U.S. Military Academy, called West Point, in Highland Falls, New York, and the U.S. Air Force Academy in Colorado Springs, Colorado); their cost per graduate ranges between $340,000 and $360,000. The difference stems primarily from two facts. The other two schools own more property on their campuses. Also, their faculty are paid twelve months of the year while USNA faculty are only paid ten months of the year.

Author's note: All of the figures in this chapter are based on accounting data for the 2002–2003 academic year. Although these figures will change, they will change at a rate proportional to other government pay changes.

Midshipman Stipend

As of 1 October 2001 the midshipman stipend was linked to the regular naval officer pay system at a rate of 35 percent of an ensign (O-1) with less than two years of service. As cost of living increases are authorized for the military, the midshipman stipend will also increase. On 1 January 2003 each midshipman grossed $764.40 per month, an amount that translates to $9,052.80 per year. Each midshipman may expect this rate to increase on par with inflation and yearly military pay raises. Midshipmen and their families pay nothing for tuition, room, board, or any kind of medical expenses including dental (not even deductibles). As members of the federal armed forces, midshipmen receive all their medical and dental care free of charge.

Each midshipman's monthly net pay, of course, is less than the $764.40 gross, considerably so in plebe and youngster years. The Academy makes numerous deductions from each midshipman's stipend. The bulk of the deductions are for large (expensive) items such as uniforms and computers. Other financial deductions are explained in detail below. The actual cash pay that midshipmen receive each month (the net amount, usually referred to as "cash pay"), and what midshipmen really care about, is easily shown in table 8.

All midshipmen are paid via direct deposit to a bank of their choice. Midshipmen have easy access to money through the Navy Federal Credit Union (NFCU), the financial institution on the Yard. Direct deposits are made on the last day of the month except when that day falls on a weekend or national holiday, in which case deposits are made on the first working day prior to the weekend or holiday (yes, it gets confusing). Along with the final direct deposit of a given month's pay, a leave and earnings statement (LES) is issued to each midshipman that describes the exact disposition of the pay for the previous month. For more information regarding military LESs, visit www.dfas.mil/money/milpay/les_djms.pdf. The LESs are also accessible through a secure military pay Web site.

Table 8. Net Monthly Stipend by Class

Class	Net Monthly Stipend
Plebe	$100.00
Youngster	$200.00
Second class	$300.00
Firstie	$400.00

```
--------------------------------------------------------------------------------
        DEFENSE  FINANCE  AND  ACCOUNTING  SERVICE  MILITARY  LEAVE  AND  EARNINGS  STATEMENT
--------------------------------------------------------------------------------
      |Name (Last, First, MI)      |SSN       |Grade|PyDate|Yrs| ETS  |Branch|ADSN PPO | Period Covered
  ID  |                            |          | C4 |000630| 03|040630| NAVY|   5197|  1-30 SEP 03
--------------------------------------------------------------------------------
         ENTITLEMENTS        |      DEDUCTIONS        |      ALLOTMENTS        |      SUMMARY
--------------------------------------------------------------------------------
    TYPE           AMOUNT|TYPE              AMOUNT|TYPE              AMOUNT|+AmtFwd     134.98
A|  BASE PAY       764.40|FEDERAL TAXES      28.51|                        |
B|                       |FICA-SOC SECURITY  47.39|                        |+Tot Ent    764.40
C|                       |FICA-MEDICARE      11.08|                        |
D|                       |STATE TAXES        13.64|                        |-Tot Ded    428.12
E|                       |SGLI FOR  250,000  16.25|                        |
F|                       |PERSONAL DEDUCT    87.55|                        |-Tot Allt      .00
G|                       |ACTIVITIES         60.00|                        |
H|                       |LUCKY BAG (YR BK)  60.00|                        |=Net Amt    471.26
I|                       |USNA STORE CHARGE 103.70|                        |
J|                       |                        |                        |-Cr Fwd      71.26
K|                       |                        |                        |
L|                       |                        |                        |------------------
M|                       |                        |                        |EOM Pay
N|                       |                        |                        |            400.00
O|                       |                        |                        |------------------
  |          |--------------------------------------------------------------|DIEMS |RetirementPlan
  |  Total   |       764.40|                                           428.12|      |
--------------------------------------------------------------------------------
       |Bf Bal|Ernd|Used| CrBal|ETSBal|Lost|Paid|UseLose|FED  |WagePeriod|  Wage YTD|Ms|Ex|  AddlTax|    Tax YTD
LEAVE| .0| .0|  0|   .0|   .0|  .0|  .0|    .0|TAXES|  764.40|  6879.60|S|01|     .00|    258.64
--------------------------------------------------------------------------------
FICA |WagePeriod|SocWageYTD| SocTaxYTD|Med Wg YTD|Med Tx YTD|STATE|St|Wg Period| Wage YTD |Ms|Ex|  Tax YTD
TAXES|  764.40|  6879.60|    426.51|  6879.60|    99.72|TAXES|VA|   764.40|  6879.60|S|01|    122.76
--------------------------------------------------------------------------------
PAY  |BAQ Type|BAQ Depn|VHA Zip| Rent Amt |Share|Sta| JFTR|Depns|2d JFTR|BAS Type| Charity|Tpc|Pacidn
DATA |        |        |       |      .00| 0 |   |    | 0|       |        |    9.99|   |
--------------------------------------------------------------------------------
THRIFT | Base P Rate|Base P Curr|Spec P Rate|Spec P Curr|Inc P Rate|Inc P Curr|Bonus P Rate|Bonus P Curr
SAVINGS|       0%           |       0%           |       0%           |      0%
PLAN   |--------------------------------------------------------------------------------
(TSP)  |                TSP YTD Deduction  | Deferred        | Exempt
       |                             .00   |        .00      |       .00
--------------------------------------------------------------------------------
  REMARKS:
      YTD ENTITLE     7056.40        YTD DEDUCT       3209.20
                     ----------                     ----------
    -ACCESS YOUR PAY ACCOUNT ONLINE AT          |SVC ACADEMY HELD PAY RELEASED        $63.72
    HTTPS://MYPAY.DFAS.MIL OR CALL 1-800-346-3374|AMOUNT DUE TO THE USNA STORE          $.00
    -SPLIT DISBURSEMENT FOR TRAVEL PAYMENTS IS  |USNA STORE CHARGE COLLECTION          (260)
    MANDATORY IF YOU USE A GOV'T TRAVEL CARD. SEE|START    ACTIVITIES      030915-030915(258)
    WWW.DFAS.MIL FOR MORE DETAILS.              |START    LUCKY BAG (YEAR 030912-030912(255)
    -RECRUITING DUTY FOR ENLISTED SERVICE MEMBERS|LAUNDRY                              $54.35
    OFFERS GREAT STATESIDE LOCATIONS AND A      |PERSONAL SERVICES                    $33.20
    MONTHLY SPECIAL DUTY ASSIGNMENT PAY. CONTACT|BANK  USAA FEDERAL SAVINGS BANK
    YOUR DETAILER TODAY.                        |
```

An example of a leave and earnings statement (LES).
Courtesy of USNA

An LES lists all deductions and withholdings. It shows federal and state income tax withholdings, as well as deductions for advance for clothing and equipment (ACE) loan repayment, gear issue items, class fund deductions, and Morale, Welfare, and Recreation (MWR) payments for items such as *The Lucky Bag,* the USNA yearbook. Standard deductions vary depending on class and sex. Female uniforms, for example, differ in price from male uniforms. See the "4/C Class of 2007—Male" chart that summarizes income, fixed deductions, variable deductions, cash pay, and balances for a fourth class male midshipman who is in the 2007 graduating class. In the chart, H/P BF denotes the held pay beginning fund balance and H/P CF denotes the held pay closing fund balance (explained below).

Each August during the fall intercessional, midshipmen are briefed on the upcoming year's budget. All midshipmen have access to an online budget book and are recommended to print it out to keep as a reference. They are advised to compare that budget with their own specific LES. Midshipmen prefer as much control over their pay as possible, so each midshipman receives a higher cash pay during the months of July and December; the increase is intended to pay for book issues for the upcoming semester.

Upon entering the Academy, midshipmen or their families must deposit about $2,200 into the midshipmen's held pay account that combines with the $6,000 ACE loan to offset the cost of initial issues during Plebe Summer. Any midshipman who does not make the initial $2,200 deposit may expect significantly lower cash pay during second and first class years.

4/C Class of 2007 - Male

	Jul	Aug	Sep	Oct	Nov	Dec	Jan	Feb	Mar	Apr	May	Jun	Year Total
INCOME													
1. H/P BF	$8,200.00	$4,067.09	$1,779.28	$1,591.62	$943.91	$1,039.25	$1,257.79	$748.23	$660.32	$878.86	$897.40	$1,115.94	
2. Stipend	$764.40	$764.40	$764.40	$764.40	$764.40	$764.40	$764.40	$764.40	$764.40	$764.40	$764.40	$764.40	$9,172.80
Sub total	$8,964.40	$4,831.49	$2,543.68	$2,356.02	$1,708.31	$1,803.65	$2,022.19	$1,512.63	$1,424.72	$1,643.26	$1,661.80	$1,880.34	
FIXED DEDUCTIONS													
3. FITW	$28.92	$28.92	$28.92	$28.92	$28.92	$28.92	$28.92	$28.92	$28.92	$28.92	$28.92	$28.92	$347.04
4. FICA	$58.47	$58.47	$58.47	$58.47	$58.47	$58.47	$58.47	$58.47	$58.47	$58.47	$58.47	$58.47	$701.64
5. SITW	$34.67	$34.67	$34.67	$34.67	$34.67	$34.67	$34.67	$34.67	$34.67	$34.67	$34.67	$34.67	$416.04
6. SGLI	$16.25	$16.25	$16.25	$16.25	$16.25	$16.25	$16.25	$16.25	$16.25	$16.25	$16.25	$16.25	$195.00
7. MIDN Services	$104.35	$87.55	$87.55	$87.55	$87.55	$87.55	$87.55	$87.55	$87.55	$87.55	$87.55	$87.55	$1,067.40
Sub total	$242.66	$225.86	$225.86	$225.86	$225.86	$225.86	$225.86	$225.86	$225.86	$225.86	$225.86	$225.86	$2,727.12
VARIABLE DEDUCTIONS													
8. Store	$2,000.00	$2,050.00	$25.00	$0.00	$0.00	$0.00	$0.00	$0.00	$0.00	$0.00	$0.00	$0.00	$4,075.00
9. Uniform	$2,367.15	$151.35	$251.20	$866.25	$121.70	$0.00	$0.00	$228.10	$281.45	$0.00	$0.00	$45.00	$4,312.20
10. Books	$187.50	$500.00	$0.00	$0.00	$0.00	$0.00	$500.00	$0.00	$0.00	$0.00	$0.00	$0.00	$1,187.50
11. MWF	$0.00	$0.00	$130.00	$0.00	$1.50	$0.00	$0.00	$0.00	$0.00	$0.00	$0.00	$0.00	$131.50
12. NAAA	$0.00	$25.00	$0.00	$0.00	$0.00	$0.00	$0.00	$25.00	$0.00	$0.00	$0.00	$0.00	$50.00
13. Alumni	$0.00	$0.00	$0.00	$0.00	$0.00	$0.00	$0.00	$0.00	$0.00	$0.00	$0.00	$0.00	$0.00
14. ACE Payment	$0.00	$0.00	$220.00	$220.00	$220.00	$220.00	$220.00	$220.00	$220.00	$220.00	$220.00	$220.00	$2,200.00
Sub total	$4,554.65	$2,726.35	$626.20	$1,086.25	$343.20	$220.00	$948.10	$526.45	$220.00	$220.00	$220.00	$265.00	$11,956.20
CASH PAY	$100.00	$100.00	$100.00	$100.00	$100.00	$100.00	$100.00	$100.00	$100.00	$300.00	$100.00	$100.00	$1,400.00
15. H/P CF	$4,067.09	$1,779.28	$1,591.62	$943.91	$1,039.25	$1,257.79	$748.23	$660.32	$878.86	$897.40	$1,115.94	$1,289.48 *	
16. ACE Balance	$6,000.00	$6,000.00	$5,780.00	$5,560.00	$5,340.00	$5,120.00	$4,900.00	$4,680.00	$4,460.00	$4,240.00	$4,020.00	$3,800.00	

* Each Midshipmen must maintain a held pay balance of at least $350 before entering 3/c year   Sea Pay**
** Sea Pay is established for uniform maintenance requirements in support of summer cruise.

An example of standard financial deductions for a plebe.
Abbreviations:

H/P BF   Held pay brought forward
FITW   Federal income tax withholding
FICA   Federal Insurance Compensation Act (Social Security and Medicare)
SITW   State income tax withheld
SGLI   Servicemember's group life insurance
MWF   Midshipman Welfare Fund
NAAA   Naval Academy Athletic Assn.
H/P CF   Held pay carried forward

The initial deposit policy is currently being reviewed; it may progress toward zero money down on I-Day and a correlative higher ACE loan.

Perks

Midshipmen enjoy a great number of financial perks including great deals on car and personal property insurance. Deals are given by the NFCU, United Services Automobile Association (USAA), Navy Mutual Aid, and Armed Forces Insurance, among others. Midshipmen receive privileges at military commissaries and exchanges. They receive discounts for many commercial activities including lodging and transportation. Midshipmen qualify for any standard military discounts that businesses offer. They also receive space-available (free) flights on military transport aircraft.

Medical Insurance

As members of the U.S. Armed Forces, midshipmen are automatically covered for all their medical and dental care. It is, in effect, free. The U.S. Navy provides or pays for all reasonable medical and dental expenses that a midshipman may incur, including emergency care received at civilian facilities. In cases requiring long-term care, midshipmen are normally transferred to a military or Veterans Affairs (VA) hospital. Sometimes, if physicians determine it necessary, midshipmen may be sent to a civilian care facility.

When an injury or illness renders a midshipman not physically qualified for commissioning, the midshipman may be separated. In this case, government financing of subsequent medical care may cease. Therefore, parental retention of medical insurance may be a good idea during a child's years at the Academy.

Contrary to most others on active duty, disabled midshipmen do not qualify for military disability pay. Also, medical benefits will likely be denied in cases involving injury caused by a midshipman's willful misconduct or negligence, notably as a result of drinking.

Financial Adviser

A supply corps officer serves as midshipmen financial adviser. This individual is responsible for the myriad financial activities listed below. He or she serves as an invaluable source of information. Each midshipman should seek the financial adviser's assistance when needed.

The financial adviser's functions include:

Preparing the annual midshipmen budget

Advising midshipmen in areas of personal finance, such as taxes, loans, real estate, investments, debt management, insurance, and car buying (Note: Adviser counsels approximately forty-five midshipmen per week in personal finance.)

Managing a four-year financial education program that brings in a nonprofit financial education foundation to teach professional financial lesson topics

Assisting in tax filing and periodically giving seminars and training to midshipmen companies

Coordinating "open houses" to introduce midshipmen to banking and insurance opportunities

As coordinator of the financial education plan, the financial adviser trains midshipmen—either individually or through seminars—to be educated and financially solvent officers. The financial education program consists of eighteen lessons during the four Academy years. It follows a curriculum that includes lessons on investing, debt management, taxes, insurance, and other pertinent financial information. Whether this training is heeded, of course, remains up to each individual midshipman.

Career Starter Loans

During the second semester of second class year, various financial institutions offer career starter loans to Naval Academy midshipmen. West Point and the Air Force Academy have similar programs. The loans are usually around $25,000, with an incredibly low 1–3 percent interest rate. The loan payback is delayed until after graduation and commissioning. Infinite uses exist for the loans: car purchasing, investments, even trips to Europe. Most midshipmen take advantage of this opportunity. Unfortunately, few are savvy investors. Therefore, many young graduates loathe the significant loan repayment that gobbles up much their paycheck as a young ensign.

Midshipmen who separate from the Academy must fully repay any loans or renegotiate them at current market lending rates.

Taxes

Midshipmen must pay income taxes, both federal and state. For their own tax purposes, parents must determine whether they can claim a midshipman as a dependent. The U.S. federal tax code is complex. Also, each state has its own codes or regulations. However, dependency rules exist that may help parents determine whether or not they may claim a midshipman as a dependent. Parents should consult their own financial adviser or the Internal Revenue Service (IRS) to help determine the dependency status of a midshipman.

A very general dependency guideline is that parents have to provide more than half the financial support for a dependent in the course of the year to claim someone as a dependent. If a midshipman can be claimed by his parents, in that same year the midshipman may *not* claim himself or herself as an exemption on his or her own tax return. In many cases, because of the level of full-year Academy pay and support, the year in which a midshipman is inducted is the only year for which a parent usually is able to claim him or her as a dependent.

–6–

Career

An SH-60B tethered to the deck of a Navy cruiser at sunset.
Author photo

For many midshipmen, service assignment (formerly called "service selection")—even more than commissioning (or graduation)—is the culminating event of their Naval Academy years. Primarily based on order of merit, but including certain subjective inputs to allow for what the Academy considers the "whole-person concept," a board of officers makes service assignments. A number of warfare communities—notably nuclear (both surface and submarine), aviation, special warfare (SEALs), Special Operations, and the combat engineering corps (CEC)—do pre-selection screening of the midshipmen they expect to be assigned at service assignment. The screening weighs primarily order of merit, medical status, and summer (or prior-enlistment) training. Traditionally, service assignment occurs in January or early February of the first class year.

Midshipmen have significantly more career options than cadets at the other service academies. Remembering that the numbers change from year to year, recent three-year averages of midshipmen selected for warfare communities are shown in table 9.

As is true for any system, some midshipmen gripe about the Academy's service assignment system. Most, however, are overwhelmingly satisfied with their assignments. Taking numbers from four years, the

Table 9. Average Numbers of Midshipmen Chosen for Various Warfare Communities

U.S. Navy Unrestricted Line	
Community	**Average Number Assigned**
Surface warfare (conventional)	215
Surface warfare (nuclear)	44
Submarine warfare	134
Pilot	244
Flight officer	87
Special warfare (SEALs)	16
Special operations	11

U.S. Marine Corps	
Community	**Average Number Assigned**
Ground	100
Pilot	49
Naval flight officer (NFO)	9

U.S. Navy Restricted Line and Staff Corps	
Community	**Average Number Assigned**
Aviation maintenance duty officer	1
Civil engineer corps	4
Cryptology	4
Human resource officer	1–2
Intelligence	4
Supply corps	9
Medical corps	14
Oceanography	0–1
Information professional	1–2

Note: The U.S. Army takes an average of 0–1 and the U.S. Air Force takes 1–2.

average percentage was found for how many midshipmen were assigned to the community they requested. As the table 10 shows, more than 98 percent earned their first or second choices in service assignments. No information is compiled that shows a correlation between a midshipman's order of merit and his or her satisfaction with service assignment. Academy officials say the following rule of thumb generally applies: the higher one's order of merit, the higher one's satisfaction with one's service assignment.

Table 10. Percentage of Midshipmen Assigned to Requested Community after Commissioning

Choice Ranking	Percentage
First	90.71
Second	7.53
Third	1.37
Fourth	0.28
Fifth	0.08
Sixth	0.00

A midshipman who, for whatever reason, is not assigned his or her first choice may usually make a lateral move to the preferred community fairly early in his or her career following receipt of an initial warfare designation (for example, after an officer earns a surface warfare designation pin). Such moves are difficult and never guaranteed. Several years of top performance in the community initially selected is required before such a transfer can even be applied for.

Service Communities

Each Navy and Marine Corps warfare community is unique. Each has its own career path, requirements for promotion, and pay incentives. The Internet hosts volumes of information on each specific community. The following information hopefully steers you to primary community Web sites to supplement the cursory introductions. A good starting point is the USNA catalog's chapter on career opportunities (www.usna.edu/Catalog/career.pdf). Like the communities themselves, no two career paths in the armed services are alike. Therefore, introductions cover only the first few years of service.

Surface Line (Conventional)

Surface warfare officers (SWOs) make up the lion's share of today's naval officers. In short, they drive ships, but in truth they do a great deal more. Most SWOs qualify as shipboard engineering officers and/or combat systems officers. Additionally, they lead the men and women on our country's naval surface vessels, stationed both at home and abroad. Performing an invaluable service, some of the best and brightest of the Academy's graduates follow this career path.

Following graduation SWOs head directly to their first ship assignment for six to ten months. Next, they go to surface warfare officer school (SWOS) in Newport, Rhode Island, for four to ten weeks of concentrated study. From there, they return to their first ship to complete their first tour of duty and their surface warfare qualification. The surface warfare designation pin is referred to as the SWO qualification pin (SWO pin for short). For more information, visit http://prodevweb.prodev.usna.edu/SWO/swocip.htm or https://www.swonet.com/cgi-bin/swoprod.dll/public.jsp.

Surface Line (Nuclear)

These officers follow similar career paths of conventional SWOs, except they have the added responsibility of running the largest and most complex naval nuclear propulsion plants in the world. Officers assigned surface nuclear duty first report to a conventional ship for a two year division officer tour so they can attain their warfighting experience and qualifications. After earning a SWO pin, the officer completes nuclear power school in Charleston, South Carolina, for six months and then nuclear prototype school either in Charleston or Balston Spa, New York, for six more months. With nuclear training complete, the officer carriers out his or her second division officer tour as a member of the reactor department on board an aircraft carrier.

Surface nuclear officers get a unique combination of both tactical and technical training on a variety of platforms early in their careers. This diversity is the key to rapid promotion in the surface warfare community. Paths can lead to command at sea, reactor officer tours, and major command.

Submarine Warfare

Submarine officers drive our nation's submarines, both attack and fleet ballistic missile submarines. In addition to leading the onboard men (women are currently not allowed to deploy on submarines), submarine officers (like their surface nuclear counterparts) also have the added responsibility of operating the ship's nuclear reactor. For this reason, their postgraduation schooling is incredibly in depth, providing them with the ability to efficiently operate reactor plants at sea in support of the submarines' wide-ranging missions, both in war and at peace. Submarine officers are usually selected from the brightest of each graduating class.

Following commissioning, officers admitted into the nuclear power program attend nuclear power school in Charleston, South Carolina, for six months. Next, they train for six more months at one of the Navy's two nuclear reactor prototypes, which are located in Charleston and Balston Spa, New York. Successful completion of these two hurdles brings the officer to Navy submarine school in New London, Connecticut, for ten weeks.

After that the officer reports to his first ship. Those assigned submarines at service assignment do not choose the submarine on which they will first serve. Toward the end of the training pipeline, personal preferences and the needs of the Navy dictate what type of submarine and homeport a young officer will be assigned. The submarine warfare designation pin, referred to as "dolphins," is typically earned between twelve and eighteen months after reporting aboard the first submarine. For more information, visit www.chinfo.navy.mil/navpalib/cno/n87/n77.html.

Note that the U.S. Navy's nuclear reactor training is provided to both submarine officers and surface nuclear officers. The nuclear power school and prototype training provide experience that is recognized and marketable both in the military and nonmilitary environments. The culmination of the nuclear training program involves a comprehensive written exam and oral interview that certifies an officer to be a naval nuclear engineering officer. This certification is equivalent to a professional engineer in the civilian world.

Naval Aviation

Navy Pilot

Navy pilots are the fliers of all naval aircraft including jets, propeller driven planes, and helicopters. Helicopter pilots account for over 50 percent of all naval aviators. In addition to flying responsibilities, pilots also lead the troops of their associated squadron. This sets them apart from Army and Air Force pilots who only fly with almost no collateral duties. A highly sought-after job, Navy pilots are further glamorized by pop culture and film. In reality, the training and subsequent flying jobs are incredibly demanding, requiring near-perfect vision, physical stamina and endurance, and mental acuity.

While at the Naval Academy, midshipmen who want to fly must be physically qualified with color-vision proficiency and 20/20 (or better) uncorrected eyesight. They must also pass a two-part, three-hour exam called the aviation selection test battery (ASTB). A test and predictor similar to the scholastic aptitude test (SAT), the ASTB measures (1) aptitude for flight school academics, (2) aptitude for flying, and (3) biographical inventory. Midshipmen failing the test must wait thirty days before trying again. Although the medical standards for Navy and Marine Corps pilots and NFOs are practically the same, the Marine Corps does have slightly more stringent standards on the ASTB.

Beginning in 1999 the Navy approved photorefractive radio keratotomy (PRK) surgery. Therefore, those desiring surgically corrected eyes and who medically qualify as a naval aviation candidate may get PRK surgery at the government's expense. If the repaired vision tests at 20/20, that midshipman may be assigned an aviation billet. Recently, an average of 175 midshipmen per year have had successful PRK surgery. This fairly recent development has dramatically changed who can be assigned to naval aviation and has caused these already highly sought-after billets to become even more so. Many who get PRK do not go to naval aviation. A midshipman electing to have the surgery in no way obligates himself or herself to the aviation community. An individual may have the surgery regardless of the sought-after service assignment.

Naval Flight Officers (NFOs)

NFOs are critical members of many aviation communities. There are no NFOs in any helicopter community. Highly trained airborne experts, NFOs serve as navigators, radar and electronic intercept officers, and antisubmarine warfare systems specialists. Like their pilot brethren, NFOs also serve myriad leadership and management positions in their squadrons. Theirs is likewise a very sought-after job. NFOs also must meet all the physical standards a pilot must meet except the standards for uncorrected eyesight.

Aviation Training

Those with billets in naval aviation (both pilot and NFO) go first to aviation preflight indoctrination (API) in Pensacola, Florida. The training lasts about six weeks.

Student naval aviators (SNAs) then either stay in Pensacola or go to Corpus Christi, Texas, for primary flight training. At the completion of primary, SNAs select their preferred aircraft type. Then, depending on the type of aircraft they will fly, SNAs complete advanced flight training in Pensacola (helicopters), Kingsville, Texas, or Meridian, Mississippi (jets), or Corpus Christi, Texas (propeller aircraft). The training track takes between eighteen to twenty-four months. Upon completion, pilots earn their warfare designation pin, which is referred to as "wings." Next the pilots head to their first fleet squadron.

Following API, NFOs remain in Pensacola for their additional training. Total training time for NFOs is twelve to eighteen months. They too earn their wings. NFO wings have two anchors crossed instead of the single anchor that appears in the naval aviator's wings. They then report to their first squadron.

There are literally countless Web sites discussing naval aviation. Begin further explorations by visiting www.naval-air.org for naval aviation history and www.navy.mil for a broad introduction to the Navy.

Naval Special Warfare (SEALs)

Naval special warfare, commonly referred to as the SEALs (Sea, Air, Land), is the U.S. Navy's elite commando unit. SEAL units exist as part of the U.S. Special Operations Command (USSOCOM) and are considered among the most elite of the country's forces. The SEALs are a relatively small community, making up only 2 percent of all naval officers (approximately 530) and are therefore one of the most selective Navy communities. Selection out of the Naval Academy is extremely competitive with only about sixteen spots awarded to each graduating class of approximately one thousand midshipmen. Naval special warfare, similar to the submarine community, is an all-male fighting force.

Training for SEALs begins at the basic underwater demolition/SEAL (BUD/S) course in Coronado, California. Divided into four phases, the course encompasses almost seven months of intense training. Upon graduation from BUD/S, officers attend static-line jump school in Fort Benning, Georgia, the junior officer training course (JOTC) in Coronado, and then SEAL qualification training (SQT). SQT is a three to four month program in which graduates earn their naval special warfare pin, referred to as the "trident." Duty stations available to SEALs include Coronado; Honolulu, Hawaii; Little Creek, Virginia; and numerous overseas duty stations. The first tour lasts three to four years. For more information, visit https://www.seal.navy.mil/.

Special Operations

Special Operations, referred to as Spec Ops, exists as the U.S. Navy's youngest unrestricted line community. Begun in 1978, Spec Ops men and women specialize in explosive ordnance disposal (EOD), underwater mine countermeasures (UMCM), and expeditionary diving and salvage. Working in all operational environments, these individuals have one primary mission objective: enabling war-fighter access. They remove ordnance and improvised explosive hazards, shallow water to surf-zone mines, and underwater wreckage that impedes expeditionary war-fighting efforts. These warriors complete the basic dive officer course en route to their first sea tour, where they will qualify to become surface warfare officers. They are then designated as Special Operations officers after completing ten to twelve months of explosive ordnance disposal (EOD) school. For more information, visit: www.bupers.navy.mil/pers2/specops/specopsnew.htm.

Marine Corps

Marines are the Department of the Navy's foot soldiers, and more. The U.S. Marine Corps has many different communities, subspecialty codes, and military operating specialties (MOSs). All, however, operate in support of the ground troops. The Marine Corps is inextricably linked to the Navy and, for this reason, many Marine Corps junior officers are Naval Academy graduates.

Up to 20 percent of any Academy class may be assigned the U.S. Marine Corps. At the time of service assignment, all who do—whether they intend to serve in a ground specialty or another capacity (aviation, for example)—choose one of about six class-up dates for The Basic School (TBS) in Quantico, Virginia. TBS lasts twenty-six weeks. Every Marine Corps officer begins his or her training at TBS. Thereafter, those in ground specialties take advanced training courses at one of many locations across the country. The durations of specialty schools vary. Those with air designations (both pilot and NFO) go to Pensacola for flight training, a training that mirrors the process for Navy aviators and NFOs (described previously). For more information, visit www.usmc.mil.

Other Specialties

All midshipmen are commissioned as unrestricted line officers, with certain exceptions. These exceptions vary, and are referred to as restricted line and staff officers. The categories include aviation maintenance duty officer (AMDO), civil engineer corps (CEC), cryptology, human resources, intelligence, supply corps, medical and dental corps, oceanography, and information professional. Additionally, no more than 1 percent of a given graduating class is allowed to select a commission in either the U.S. Army or U.S. Air Force. For these communities the career path begins with training in the chosen field, after which the path changes dramatically.

Obligation

All newly commissioned naval ensigns or U.S. Marine Corps second lieutenants serve a minimum of five years, except (1) Navy pilots serve eight years following receipt of their wings, (2) Navy NFOs serve seven years following receipt of their wings, (3) Marine Corps pilots serve eight years following receipt of their wings, and (4) Marine Corps NFOs serve six years following receipt of their wings.

Temporary assigned duty (TAD), the duty new Academy graduates often serve while awaiting the beginning of their warfare school, is not included in service obligation times. Initial TAD does, however, extend the period of total service for those in aviation because their years of obligation do not begin until receipt of their wings. Anyone failing to complete specialized training, such as nuclear power school, flight school, or BUD/S—regardless of the reason—continues his or her service obligation in whatever other part of the Navy or Marine Corps that may be assigned.

Pay and Incentives

Different communities pay handsomely for their specifically trained officers. These numbers get incredibly confusing, however, because they differ based on rank, time in service, specialty codes, and duration in a respective community.

For up-to-date pay information, visit the Defense Finance and Accounting Service's Web site (www.dfas.mil/money/milpay). Current military pay scales are posted there with lists of specific communities and their corresponding pay incentives.

-7-

Briefer Points

A great deal of information about the U.S. Naval Academy does not fit neatly into any particular category. In this chapter you will find an alphabetical listing of incredibly diverse topics.

Academy Organization

The highest ranking individual at the Naval Academy, the equivalent of a civilian college president, is the Superintendent. The Superintendent is selected for the post by the Secretary of the Navy.

The Superintendent (referred to as the "Supe" by midshipmen) is a flag rank officer (meaning, simply, very high-ranking), now usually at least a three-star rear admiral. Directing the entire Academy operation, the Super-

Every year at graduation, the Blue Angels fly spectacular air shows in Annapolis. Shown here flying over the graduation stadium itself.
Courtesy of USNA

intendent oversees a more than $100 million annual Academy budget and reports to the Secretary of the Navy and the Chief of Naval Operations (who reports to the Secretary of Defense, who reports to the

Commander-in-Chief—the President). For more information on the Superintendent, visit www.usna.edu/PAO/supesoff.html.

By law the Academy's oversight body is the Board of Visitors, which meets several times a year. Its members are appointed by Congress and the president. Those appointed by Congress are members of the Senate and the House of Representatives. The Superintendent also has six major assistants. The two most notable are the Commandant and the Academic Dean and Provost.

The Commandant is referred to as the "Dant" by midshipmen. A senior Navy captain or Marine Corps colonel, the Commandant has duties that partly approximate those of a civilian college dean of students. In addition, as commander of the Brigade, the Dant oversees discipline and military training. Because of this, the Commandant certainly has a more direct effect on the daily lives of midshipmen than the Superintendent does. For more information on the Commandant, visit www.usna.edu/Commandant.

The Academic Dean and Provost is a civilian who presides over the curriculum and the six-hundred-plus faculty members. The Academic Dean serves as the Superintendent's top adviser in all academic matters. For more information on the Academic Dean, visit www.nadn.navy.mil/AcDean/staff/staff.html.

In addition, the Superintendent receives input from two permanent boards—the Board of Visitors and the Objectives Review Board (ORB). Perhaps foremost is the ORB, whose members include the Commandant and Academic Dean, the directors of the four academic divisions, and other key officials. The ORB meets regularly to consider major matters of policy, but it has an unlimited charter. To further explore the Academy's organization, visit www.usna.edu/admin.htm.

Addresses

U.S. Mail

Every midshipman at the Academy gets his or her own post office box. The same box number is kept for the duration of each midshipman's stay. The Academy's post office, which contains not only forty-five hundred post office boxes but also a customer service desk like all other U.S. post offices, is located in the basement of Bancroft Hall's eighth wing. Following Plebe Summer, mail should be addressed to a midshipman in the following manner:

Midn 4/C Joe Mid
P.O. Box 12345
Annapolis, MD 21412

To confuse matters, mail sent to brand new plebes during Plebe Summer must also include a the midshipman's company and platoon number because that mail is handled slightly differently. Therefore, mail sent to a plebe during Plebe Summer should be addressed in the following manner:

Midn 4/C Joe Mid
YY Company ZZ Platoon
P.O. Box 12345
Annapolis, MD 21412

Non–U.S. Postal Service Mail

Non–U.S. Postal Service mail includes deliveries from UPS (United Parcel Service), Federal Express, DHL, Airborne, and other carriers. Mail sent by any carrier other than the U.S. Postal Service must be sent to the Naval Academy's Express Office. In our post–September 11th world, this measure is for the security of the midshipmen. Addressing requirements, likewise, are different. The fundamental difference is the omission of a specific midshipman's P.O. box number. Therefore, the address for all carriers other than the U.S. Postal Service is as follows:

Midn 4/C Joe Mid
Company XX
Bancroft Hall/Express Office
U.S. Naval Academy
Annapolis, MD 21412

For ease of pick-up by midshipmen, parcel post service via the U.S. Postal Service is usually preferable to any non–U.S. Postal Service carriers.

E-mail

E-mail is the primary form of communication between midshipmen and their friends and family. Each midshipman is given an e-mail address that corresponds to his or her alpha code in this way:

m123456@usna.edu

The numbers are the midshipman's alpha code. Furthermore, many mid-shipmen keep e-mail addresses they had prior to becoming a midshipman (for example, hotmail, msn, yahoo, aol).

Alcohol

See "Drugs and Alcohol" section in this chapter.

Alumni Association

The U.S. Naval Academy Alumni Association is a private, independent, and nonprofit organization. Today's alumni house is the former Ogle Hall, a pre-Revolutionary (1739) building two blocks from Gate 3, located at the corner of King George Street and College Avenue.

According to the Alumni Association:

The U.S. Naval Academy Alumni Association and the United States Naval Academy Foundation [see "Foundation" section in this chapter] are two independent, not-for-profit, corporations sharing a single President/Chief Executive Officer and operating as a fully integrated organization in support of the Naval Academy and its mission.

The mission of the Alumni Association is to serve and support the United States, the Naval Service and the Naval Academy and its alumni by furthering the highest standards at the Naval Academy. It does this by seeking out, informing, and encouraging qualified young men and women to pursue careers as officers in the Navy and Marine Corps.

The Alumni Association communicates issues to its members through its Web site, www.usna.com, e-mail, and *Shipmate* magazine. The association also provides its members with a variety of services, including sponsorship of events around the country; class, chapter and parent club support; career transition assistance; a welcome tent at home football games; a travel program; and much more.

All current and former midshipmen are eligible for regular membership. Anyone who has demonstrated active support of the Naval Academy or the Alumni Association may be invited to apply for Associate Membership. For more information about the Alumni Association, please visit www.usna.com.

Annapolis (the Town)

Annapolis is steeped in history and traditions that date to 1649 when it was founded by Puritans who had been driven out of Virginia by intolerant Anglicans. Few contemporary American cities can boast a more distinguished history.

Today downtown Annapolis is a National Historic Site full of outstanding Georgian and colonial architecture, including the Paca House, the Chase-Lloyd House, and the Hammond-Harwood House that stand close to the Academy, and the Charles Carroll of Carrollton House that stands several blocks farther away. Since its inception, Annapolis has continued to be a busy port, combining a working waterfront with thousands of pleasure boats, both power and sail.

Annapolis is the capital of Maryland, as well as the seat of Anne Arundel County. There are approximately thirty-five thousand people in Annapolis proper; the surrounding areas of Severna Park, Arnold, Edgewater, and Cape St. Claire boost this number significantly. Annapolis boasts a diverse and vibrant culture, numerous boutiques and galleries, extensive lodging, and hundreds of restaurants. For a complete list of everything commercial Annapolis has to offer, visit the Annapolis Chamber of Commerce Web site at www.annapolischamber.com. Annapolis also (obviously) boasts the U.S. Naval Academy, founded on the city's Windmill Point in 1845. The city's dock (referred to as City Dock) is two blocks from Gate 1 and five blocks from Gate 3.

Washington, D.C., is thirty-five miles due west. Baltimore is thirty-five miles north. Maryland's rural Eastern Shore (with towns such as St. Michael's, Oxford, and Easton) lies a few miles east, across the Chesapeake Bay Bridge.

Annapolis has it all. It would be hard to imagine a town with more charm, or with more hospitality for midshipmen. Visit www.ci.annapolis.md.us and www.visit-annapolis.org for general information on the city of Annapolis.

Army-Navy Game

The Army-Navy game is considered by many to be the great collegiate football game of the year. Nearly all midshipmen and West Point cadets are required to attend. The Naval Academy Athletic Association (NAAA) sells tickets to the game separately from season-ticket packages (see "Tickets" section in this chapter).

Most Army-Navy games are played in Philadelphia; some are played elsewhere, including the Meadowlands and Baltimore. The schedulers seek to slate one game outside Philadelphia in every midshipman's (or cadet's) four-year career.

If you get the chance, run—don't walk—to one of these games! While the football itself may leave something to be desired, the experience will be one you'll always remember.

Blue and Gold Officers

The official name of Blue and Gold Officers is Naval Academy Information Officers. The candidate guidance office coordinates a nationwide network of about twelve thousand of them. These officers, located in every state, are trained to be well qualified to counsel hopeful applicant candidates on all aspects of the U.S. Naval Academy. Each candidate is required to be formally interviewed by a Blue and Gold Officer prior to an offer of appointment. Following each interview, the Blue and Gold Officer writes a report for consideration by the Admissions Board.

Boat Shows

Each year, Annapolis hosts two massive boat shows in the fall that draw thousands upon thousands to quaint little Annapolis. All of the downtown City Dock area (only blocks from the Naval Academy) is altered to accommodate the hoards. The city builds temporary docks and erects fences; traffic flow is redirected. And usually, the shows are only one week apart: sailboats first, then powerboats. For more specific information about these shows, visit www.usboat.com.

During "boat show weekends," as the locals call them, a hotel room cannot be secured unless very preliminary reservations have been made. Everyone waits incredibly long amounts of time for dinner tables. Expect to be frustrated by traffic and parking delays. Now imagine how much worse it can be when one (or both) of these boat shows coincides with a home Navy football game. Proper preparation for these particular weekends is critical.

Care Packages

Midshipmen love mail. They love mail they can eat even more. In care packages include what the midshipman will want or need. Do not put in what is not allowed. Snacks and such, particularly for plebes, are almost always welcome: brownies, cereal, crackers, chips, cookies, soups, and small containers of juice. So are quarters for the vending machines. For the most part, follow the midshipman's desires and requests. Furthermore, to limit the population of mice and other unwanted occupants of Bancroft Hall, all food must be kept in hard plastic containers. Sending food in these containers (Tupperware, etc.) is advisable.

For ease of pick-up by midshipmen, parcel post (U.S. Postal Service) is preferable to United Parcel Service (UPS) or other non–U.S. Postal Service carriers. See "Addresses" section in this chapter.

Cars, Motorcycles, and Bicycles

Cars

Firsties may own and drive a car anywhere, including on the Yard if the appropriate decals are displayed correctly.

Second class may keep a car at the USNA stadium. They may drive their cars when departing on or returning from authorized leave. They may also drive when in uniform to and from the Yard for certain Academy functions and during Ring Dance weekend.

Youngsters and plebes may not keep a car anywhere near the Academy. They are not allowed to drive a car anywhere near the Academy except when on leave.

The Academy has no rules pertaining to car rentals. Assuming midshipmen are of the age stipulated by a given rental company for rental, they enjoy the same discounts on cars as active duty service personnel.

Motorcycles

Naval Academy regulations stipulate that unless possessing permission, which is extraordinarily rare, from the Commandant, no midshipman may own, operate, or ride a motorcycle, moped, or motor-driven bicycle. Period.

Bicycles

Midshipmen may ride bicycles. Those on the cycling or triathlon teams may keep their bikes on the Yard. Other midshipmen wishing to use their bikes for workout purposes may keep their bikes in a storage room if they have secured approval from their chain of command. They may ride their bikes to and from the Yard when they have town liberty.

Cemetery

The cemetery dates from the late 1860s. It is between six and seven acres. It contains about five thousand burial sites, with only about two hundred remaining. Those eligible for cemetery burial are:

Any military person (including enlisted) on active duty at the Academy at the time of death

Spouses and stillborn or infant children (under seven years old) of those on active duty at the Academy

Flag rank Academy graduates if flag rank was earned while on active (not reserve) duty

Unremarried spouses of anyone already buried there

Anyone in the U.S. Navy or U.S. Marine Corps whose spouse is already buried there

There also exists a newer Columbarium. It has about twenty-five hundred niches that can accommodate up to five thousand urns. Those eligible for interment in the Columbarium are:

Any U.S. Naval Academy graduate and his/her spouse

Any Naval Academy graduate's unmarried spouse if the graduate died before his or her spouse.

Any Naval Academy graduate's child (under seven years old).

A spouse who predeceases the graduate may be interred in the Columbarium; however, that act obligates the graduate to be interred there as well, even if he or she remarries. Space in the cemetery and Columbarium is limited. Ultimate decisions may fall to the Superintendent or the Secretary of the Navy.

Church

See "Worship" section in this chapter.

Class Rings, Pins, etc.

Each class, via committee, designs its own class crest during plebe year. In the fall of youngster year, members of the class are offered the opportunity to buy class crest pins, charms, stick pins, tie tacks, tie bars, and cuff links. The items are first available in late spring of each year, but they remain on sale at the Midshipmen Store and elsewhere for the next three years.

A second class and his date admire his new class ring at the annual Ring Dance.
Courtesy of USNA

Class rings come later. Around Christmas of youngster year, the process of ring selection begins: size, fit, finish, gold content, type of stone or plug in the center, special designs—whatever. Cost ranges from several hundred dollars to several thousand, depending on a great many variables. There are two primary companies that supply U.S. Naval Academy class rings: Jostens (www.jostens.com) and Herff Jones (www.herff-jones.com). Some midshipmen purchase stones from local Annapolis jewelers, other trusted family jewelers, or online and then insert them into their class rings when they arrive.

The rings are not available until the spring of second class year. Midshipmen are not allowed to wear the class rings until the Ring Dance in late May. At that dance, the ring is dipped into a binnacle that supposedly contains water from the seven seas. Tradition holds that the ring's Academy seal is worn facing outward and the class crest facing inward until commissioning. After commissioning, the ring is turned around and the sides are thus reversed. Class rings are available in miniature versions, which some midshipmen use as engagement rings. Additionally, a very small percentage of female midshipmen purchase a miniature for them-selves instead of the female version of the class ring because they prefer it.

Because class rings are expensive, midshipmen should get insurance on them. Most midshipmen, however, at this point in their lives do not have any personal property insurance. Parents may want to remind their midshipman of the importance of insurance for high value items.

Any midshipman who graduates from the Academy is authorized to own a class ring. Even though there is no stipulation stating that graduat-ing midshipmen must purchase a ring, he or she will have to explain the reason for not purchasing one to the Deputy Commandant, something that may intimidate many midshipmen. Furthermore, any midshipman separated from the Academy must return his or her ring. If a midshipman claims a ring is "lost," he or she must produce an insurance claim and a host of other paperwork. The Academy does not want anyone who did not graduate to have a ring. Period.

Color Company

During the academic year, each company and its members receive points for many aspects of Academy life—academics, athletics, and military per-formance. The company garnering the most points becomes the color com-pany for the next academic year. The winning company's members receive consequent privileges, such as parking their cars on the Yard in special areas (for firsties only), special liberty during Commissioning Week, and complimentary travel (as a company) to one away football game.

At the Color Parade during Commissioning Week, when the results of the year's competition are announced, a friend or the fiancée of the winning company's company commander—designated as the color per-son—transfers the flag from the old color company to the new.

Until recently, the color person was the "color girl." The name was officially changed in anticipation of the day when the company com-mander will be a female; therefore her friend or fiancé will be male. Problems will arise, however, because traditionally the color person is inducted into a society of former color girls, for which there are celebra-tions, secret handshakes, and the like. Also, a traditional gift to each new color person is a string of pearls.

It is an honor to be the company commander during the Color Parade. Tradition has been that the commander who leads the company during the parade is the fall semester company commander. The person who ulti-mately makes this call, however, is the color company's Company Officer. A

The color person (here a female) is escorted by the Superintendent during the annual Color Parade during Commissioning Week.
Courtesy of USNA

recent case involved a fall semester company commander who became plagued with conduct trouble late in his firstie year. For this reason, the Company Officer determined that the spring semester company commander, who had remained conduct trouble free, was more deserving of the job.

Commands

The U.S. Naval Academy is one of a number of Annapolis area Navy and Marine Corps commands. The one most closely tied to the Academy is Naval Station Annapolis—a subordinate command of the Academy's

Superintendent. The role of the naval station is to support the Academy in various ways. It provides the Academy with personnel, services, and material. Located across the Severn River from the Academy, the naval station has a Navy exchange, a commissary, and other services for Navy and Marine Corps personnel. The Academy golf course is located at the naval station, as are shooting ranges for midshipmen training and the five-hundred-foot radio towers at Greenbury Point (now inoperative and only preserved as osprey nesting areas). The naval station also houses the Marine Corps contingent that performs guard duty at the Academy, including at the gates to the Yard and at the chapel crypt of John Paul Jones. For more information about the naval station at Annapolis, visit www.usna.edu/NavalStation/newpage.htm.

Commissioning Week

Commissioning Week is the culmination of four years by the bay. If you are a parent or otherwise lucky enough to be invited, attend as many of the scheduled events as possible.

Commissioning Week begins on a Saturday in May with the Ring Dance. A very rough outline of the schedule of major events is:

Saturday	Ring Dance
Sunday	Baccalaureate
Monday	Dedication Parade; Plebe Recognition Ceremony (Herndon)
Tuesday	Blue Angels practice flight
Wednesday	Blue Angels flight demonstration; graduation ball
Thursday	Color Parade; Prizes and Awards Ceremony
Friday	Commissioning Ceremony/graduation

There are other ceremonies, briefings, tours, parties, receptions, and staged pictures. Activities change from year to year and many depend on a particular midshipman's accomplishments. In short, Commissioning Week is a wonderfully crazy time filled with relief (on the part of both families and midshipmen alike) as well as unbelievable celebration.

Some noteworthy points of interest follow. Parents and/or friends of newly commissioned officers pin on the new ranks of ensign or second lieutenant. Tradition has been that newly commissioned officers must deliver a silver dollar to the first person who salutes him or her. Children crave midshipmen covers. Following the hat toss, young kids storm the field to collect as many as they can carry. The Blue Angels' performances are spectacular. Oftentimes, the practice show on Tuesday is a better show than the "real" show the following day. Also, because the show is dependent upon weather, there is no guarantee that either will take place.

Amid much celebration exists the possibility of excess celebration. If midshipmen cross the lines of conduct—even during Commissioning Week—they may face steep penalties. The worst would be not graduating. This has happened. Midshipmen must exercise caution even while celebrating.

Commissioning Week gobbles up all available Annapolis lodging just as the home football games and boat shows do. Prudent parents make arrangements early—even several years early. Frequently, parents and families of midshipmen rent houses that are not usually used for lodging. The logic is that local Annapolitans don't really care for the madness of Commissioning Week. Many leave town and open up their homes for rental, often for thousands of dollars per week, a sum that may actually pay for their vacation. While steep, the price is worth it to allow places (even floor space) for distant relatives and friends of graduates. Information on rental properties exists in many different places: area businesses, sponsor family recommendations, *Annapolis Capital* ads, *Trident* newspaper ads, and online. Midshipmen are an invaluable source of information in this effort; they frequently find names of places from friends and acquaintances in classes above their own. Other invaluable sources of information are parents organizations (see "Parents Organizations" section in this chapter).

Many people who have witnessed one or more Commissioning Weeks—both as spectators and participants—usually note two primary downsides to the festivities: the heat and the crowds. The heat can be unbearable; plan accordingly. Most family members and friends drive to Annapolis. The result is unbelievable parking nightmares and traffic jams. The families of the approximately one thousand graduates are all prouder than anyone can possibly imagine. Everyone wants to be part of the action. Be patient. Carpool when possible. Walk when possible. Don't get frustrated. It's supposed to be a happy time, not one filled with aggravation.

Oh, and gifts *are* in order. Generally, gifts may include officer swords, custom uniforms, jewelry, U.S. Marine Corps uniforms, or anything deemed appropriate. Remember that no midshipman—nor his family—has had to pay for his or her college education. This may be a time to use some of the money saved on a very nice gift.

The crypt of John Paul Jones, located beneath the U.S. Naval Academy Chapel.
Courtesy of USNA

The Crypt

John Paul Jones's remains are beneath the Naval Academy Chapel. It is a sacred, surreal place that is guarded by Marines and demands reverence. For information on Crypt hours and tours, visit www.navyonline.com or call 410-263-6933.

Dating

Considering the Academy as a typical college, the students are no different. They date one another. But because the Academy is a very different kind of college, dating, like many Academy nuances, has rules.

Plebes may date each other, unless both plebes are in the same company. Plebes may date civilians—even the civilians they dated prior to I-Day, though it takes a special kind of relationship to survive four years by the bay. See *2% Club* entry in the Midspeak dictionary (Chapter 8).

Upperclass may not date plebes, nor may plebes date upperclass. Upperclass may date other upperclass, unless both upperclass are in the same company.

Because some people believe that you can't control whom you fall in love with, midshipmen sometimes date members of their same company, which is against the rules. When this happens, whether it be two plebes or two upperclass, one of the offending parties must move companies. The means by which this occurs is called a "love chit." The couple must submit a request chit admitting their affection and subsequent desire to have one of them move companies. Upon approval, the Company Officer finds one member of the couple a new home so the relationship can continue. This is called accommodating (the pun is intentional).

Public displays of affection (PDA) by midshipmen in uniform, on or off the Yard, are not acceptable—just as they are not acceptable in the fleet. Midshipmen may escort members of the opposite sex by having the male offer his arm to the female, regardless of who is in uniform.

The Day's Daily Routine

The Naval Academy has six academic class periods each day, with no classes on Saturdays or Sundays. There are also lab periods, periods that last longer than others, and special weeks when there are seven class periods in a day to allow for non-classtime exams. See *X-period* and *X-week* entries in the Midspeak dictionary (Chapter 8). People wake up at a variety of different times and likewise go to bed at a variety of different times, sometimes based on their class year. More specifics are not given here because of the nature of change at the Academy. For example, there has been discussion of moving to a seven-period day. Midshipmen usually share their schedule with family members and friends.

Drugs and Alcohol

Drugs are a zero-tolerance no-no. They are also illegal. In accordance with Navy-wide regulations and practices, midshipmen are subject to random urinalysis for the detection of drugs. Expulsion is the likely consequence for illegal drug use.

Regarding alcohol, the Academy adheres strictly to Maryland's drinking age law. Midshipmen must be twenty-one to purchase or consume alcohol. The Academy also encourages responsible alcohol use and severely punishes cases of abuse or misuse. Plebes (even those who are twenty-one) may not drink except when away from the Academy on leave. Upperclassmen may drink in appropriate places if they are twenty-one. Except when and where authorized by the Commandant, drinking is not permitted anywhere on the Yard (aside from in the Officers' Club). Drinking in Bancroft Hall is never permitted.

Extracurricular Activities (ECAs)

The Academy has over seventy ECAs. They range from publications to academic and athletic clubs, from musical/theatrical groups to military and professional societies, from recreational and religious organizations to social service ones. For a complete list, visit www.usna.edu/MidActivities/activity.html.

To participate in an ECA, midshipmen must have a 2.0 or higher average. All ECAs except honor societies must have at least twenty members. There is also a category within the category. Certain ECAs, such as the drum and bugle corps, cheerleaders, and the cannoneers, are designated Brigade support activities. They are exempt from some drill and intramural sports requirements. Other ECAs are not exempt. Generally, ECAs may meet only on Tuesdays and Thursdays between 6:30 and 8:00 PM.

Facilities

The facilities on the Yard are extensive. The hours of operation for particular gates and various buildings change frequently as do security measures at the Academy that are based on current global and geopolitical activities. For the most current and accurate information, visit the Naval Academy's visitor center Web site at www.navyonline.com. Also see "Tours" section in this chapter.

FONA

In the post–September 11th world, security is a primary issue at every military installation worldwide including the Naval Academy. That said, any person can access the Naval Academy Yard provided he or she has a current photo ID. Driving on the Yard, however, is a different story.

In order to drive on the Yard, a vehicle must either have Department of Defense (DOD) decals or a Friends of the Naval Academy (FONA) pass. The Academy provides these passes primarily to sponsors and parents of midshipmen. All parents of midshipmen may obtain a FONA pass through their midshipman. Parents or sponsors who already have DOD decals do not require FONA passes as well. A midshipman submits the original pass request through his or her chain of command and the Academy will mail the pass to the parent or sponsor. Incoming plebes fill the form out prior to I-Day and the passes are generally issued shortly thereafter (but usually just before I-Day). In past years the Academy has authorized a candidate's acceptance letter as a pass if the FONA pass has not yet arrived. The letter must match the ID of the person in the vehicle.

Rules associated with FONA passes are:

The passes are specific to a given vehicle and are not interchangeable. Passes that do not match the driver and/or vehicle likely will be seized at the gate.

If a parent will be driving a rental car, the FONA pass must specify "rental" in the vehicle identification area on the pass. Parents are also required to have a valid rental agreement with them as they present the pass at the gate.

Parents who obtain a FONA pass for their personal vehicle may not use it for a rental vehicle; a separate pass must be obtained that specifies "rental."

Replacements and renewals may be obtained by filling out a form and faxing or mailing it to the USNA Pass and ID Office. E-mail will not suffice because a signature is required.

Football

Football and football games are the Academy's big money maker. They are also a lot of fun regardless of the team's performance. Following are several important points about games.

Arrive at the stadium well in advance of the game—in time to see both the march-over and the march-on. Those arriving after the march-over, for which all nearby traffic is stopped, will encounter significant traffic jams and will have even greater difficulty getting into both the parking lot and the stadium itself.

Post–September 11th security is a reality. For this reason, expect bags to be searched. There is no readmittance if you depart the stadium.

All midshipmen attend every home game unless they (1) have duty or (2) are away from the Academy on a sanctioned movement order or approved liberty/leave. All midshipmen must march on to the game except for very few exceptions. Also, no midshipman is allowed to leave the stadium prior to the game's end, including during halftime.

Only first class midshipmen are allowed to sit with parents and friends in the stands. For this to happen, however, the midshipman must buy an additional ticket. The required Brigade seating area ticket, however, is not redeemable. All other midshipmen must sit with the Brigade. Often the best way to see a particular midshipman during the game is to arrange to meet at an agreed place during halftime.

Both National Collegiate Athletic Association (NCAA) and Academy rules prohibit alcohol sales in the stadium. Possession of alcohol in the stands is not allowed either. Officials check for possession at the entrance gates.

In the interest of building spirit, upperclass midshipmen often "bet" with plebes on the outcome of football games for nonmonetary stakes. Plebes, of course, must always bet on Navy, which in recent years has been a losing bet.

Foundation

The Foundation's official name is the U.S. Naval Academy Foundation, Inc. It is connected to the Naval Academy Alumni Association in that the president of the alumni association is also the president of the foundation. According to the foundation:

> The mission of the Foundation is to provide the means and the incentives for alumni, parents and friends to contribute private funds for programs at the Naval Academy, which will directly contribute to the enhancement of the highest levels of excellence in all areas of the Academy's mission and for which appropriated funds are not available. The Naval Academy Athletic and Scholarship Program, a division of the United States Naval Academy Foundation, encourages and supports athletic excellence at the Naval Academy. The program is responsible for sponsoring up to 80 top candidates each year through a year of prep school before they enter the Naval Academy. This program recognizes that superiority in athletics coupled with a comprehensive academic program will ensure that the Naval Academy has the best scholar-athletes in the nation.

Also see "Alumni Association" section in this chapter.

Giving

The Academy has a number of entities that will gladly accept tax-deductible contributions. You can specify your gift to athletics, academics, the museum, and many other possibilities. The best way to determine the extent of these possibilities is to contact the Naval Academy Alumni Association or visit the association's Web site at www.usna.com.

Herndon

Officially the Plebe Recognition Ceremony, the event is rarely referred to as that. It's Herndon. And any parent or friend of a plebe ought to see it.

What happens is this. In late May, early in Commissioning Week, the plebe class rushes from Bancroft Hall to the Herndon monument near the front of the chapel. Upperclass have greased the twenty-one-foot obelisk with lard, crankcase grease, and whatever else they can imagine. At the top they have fixed—even taped and/or fused—a Dixie-cup sailor's hat.

Only when one of the plebes replaces the Dixie cup with a midshipman's cover do plebes shuck the word "plebe" and become officially members of the fourth class. The distinction lasts only a short time—until commissioning of the firsties. No sooner do the (now former) firsties toss their covers into the air than the (former) fourth class slap on their youngster shoulder boards.

Teamwork is essential to conquer the Herndon monument.
Courtesy of USNA

The Herndon monument was erected in 1859 in memory of CDR William Herndon, who went down two years earlier with the mail steamer *Central America* in a storm off Cape Hatteras. Some time before 1900, plebes began celebrating the end of fourth class year by rushing from Dahlgren Hall to Herndon. They began climbing the monument around 1957.

The first recorded time occurred in 1962, when the class of 1965 accomplished the task in three minutes. The fastest time so far has been one minute, thirty seconds, accomplished in 1969 by the class of 1972. The slowest time so far has been four hours, twelve minutes, seventeen seconds in 1995 by the class of 1998.

History

Previous editions of this book had an entire chapter devoted to the history of the Academy and the Yard. In preparation for this edition, however, this chapter was not included for a variety of reasons. Because there exist so many fantastic resources describing the Naval Academy's history in tremendous detail, any attempt to paraphrase this rich, remarkable history would actually do the reader a disservice, not a favor.

To learn more about the history of the Naval Academy, begin research by taking the virtual tour at the Academy's Web site. The tour breaks down the highlights of history into decades, beginning with the 1840s. Visit www.usna.edu/VirtualTour/150years.

I-Day

I-Day is the shortened term for Induction Day. Make plans to attend! Unless you live near Annapolis and can drive to the Academy that morning, family members and friends should arrive at least the night before with the individual being inducted. Stay in an Annapolis hotel, motel, or a bed and breakfast (B&B) inn. Some parents' organizations recommend arriving an entire day beforehand to acquaint parents and the new plebe with the Yard and the town. Whenever you arrive, celebrate! It will be the new plebe's last chance to do that for a while.

Be on time the morning of I-Day. The day is a milestone in the inductee's life, even if the midshipman does not believe this at certain trying times. After the new plebe disappears into (usually) Alumni Hall, family members and friends spend the rest of the day waiting for the induction ceremony in Tecumseh Court (T-Court) that begins about

Induction ceremony in Tecumseh Court on I-Day.
Courtesy of USNA

6 PM. While waiting, many roam the Yard and get a feel for the place. In the process, they may catch a glimpse of their new plebe. Sometimes, top Academy officials hold briefings for parents throughout the day. The schedule of events you receive that day will describe the opportunities and locations. Additionally, sometimes officials set up televisions that show videos and live coverage of I-Day processing.

The weather is usually incredibly and almost unbearably hot. Bring a lot of film and/or video recorders, a lot of Kleenex, maybe some reading, and a cooler (without alcohol). Family and friends may also want to bring a drink (water) and snack for the midshipman. He or she may not have eaten much during the day. And get to T-Court well in advance of the induction ceremony's appointed hour to ensure that you can see.

The procedure following the ceremony is for parents to gather on Stribling Walk at the letter corresponding with the first letter of their last name, to which the new midshipman will come at induction's end.

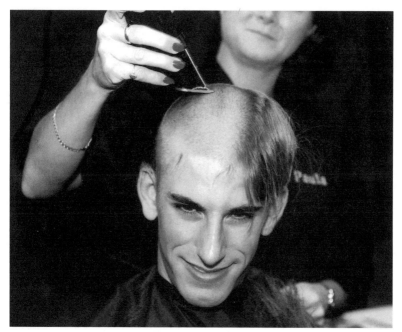

All males get their heads shaved on I-Day; most are not happy about it.
Courtesy of USNA

Inductee and family and friends will have about twenty minutes together. That's all. You'll probably cry, and your new midshipman may as well, though he or she will try to resist it. And while the new midshipman will want to say goodbye, he or she will probably be thinking about other upcoming things. It's best if family members and friends don't feel needy and squeeze out the last few seconds. When the midshipman says it's time to leave, let him or her leave with dignity.

Most midshipmen, parents, family members, and friends are concerned about the yelling that is known to take place whenever someone enters any branch of the U.S. Armed Forces. Yelling at the Academy does not *officially* begin until day four or five of Plebe Summer. The first few days are the processing phase. Plebes learn to shape up their rooms, take placement exams, fill out paperwork, and receive in-briefs. After these processes are complete, the detailers shift to other companies. Then the real training begins.

A new plebe says good-bye on Stribling Walk following the induction ceremony.
Courtesy of USNA

Liberty and Leave

See "Liberty and Leave" section in Chapter 3.

Mail

See "Addresses" section in this chapter.

Medical and Dental

As members of the federal armed forces, midshipmen receive all their medical and dental care free of charge. The medical and dental facilities are scattered throughout the Yard. Some clinics are housed in Bancroft Hall. Sick call is several times daily for diagnosis and treatment. The medical staff and numerous visiting specialists also see midshipmen for routine check-ups, annual physicals, physical therapy, screenings, immunizations, ortho-pedics, acute care, and other specialized care needs. The dental staff gives annual exams, cleanings, and fluoride treatments. They also provide just

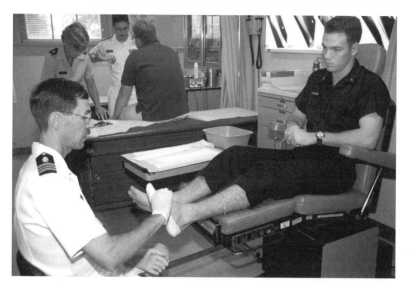

A Navy doctor examines a midshipman's sore foot.
Courtesy of USNA

about all aspects of dental medicine, including oral surgery and limited orthodontics. Dental staff sees patients either at morning and afternoon sick call Monday through Friday, or by appointment. A duty crew for both medical and dental remains available twenty-four hours a day.

Emergency patients are taken to Anne Arundel Medical Center in Annapolis or to Baltimore depending on the type of care required. Serious long-term cases are treated within the Navy's hospital system, usually at the National Naval Medical Center in Bethesda, Maryland, near Washington, D.C.

Additionally, if a midshipman requires emergency medical care while on liberty or leave, he or she should seek that care at any nearby medical facility. After completing paperwork, the cost will be covered by the military medical insurance system if the need was a "bona fide" emergency.

Many parents retain their own health insurance coverage on their midshipman in addition to what the military provides. The reason for this is that an unpredictable and unforeseen medical discharge from the Academy may render medical insurance after discharge—because of an unforeseen condition—impossible to find. Yes, it seems a slim chance,

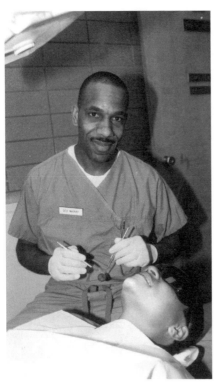

Navy dental service is given with a smile.
Courtesy of USNA

but to ensure continuous health care insurance coverage for their children, many parents believe the price is worthwhile.

The Midshipmen Store (Midstore)

Located in the basement of Bancroft Hall's first and third wings, the Naval Academy's Midshipmen Store, primarily called the Midstore by midshipmen, dates from 1867. It is the primary place where midshipmen do their shopping. It is an incredibly large store that offers everything most major department stores offer, and then some.

The Midstore has well over thirty-five thousand items—from snacks to sodas, from books to stereos, from T-shirts and running shoes to soap and socks. In addition, it has the largest selection of, and the best prices on, Navy/USNA-imprinted clothing and gifts anywhere. It also offers such services as special orders, engraving, and film developing. The store is open to all those who have a Midstore shopping card, including USNA faculty and staff, and to the immediate families of midshipmen.

Store hours, published at www.usna-store.com, tend to change based on a variety of reasons. For example, special hours are observed during home football games, Commissioning Week, and homecoming. The store closes during certain vacation periods and on weekends except during special events.

Midstore sales can exceed $12 million annually. Net proceeds are returned to the Brigade and are used to help fund numerous activities and club sports for the midshipmen.

Near the Midstore are other establishments offering goods and services for the exclusive use of midshipmen and Academy-related personnel. In Bancroft's basement, there is the cobbler shop, the tailor shop, the barber and beauty shop, a laundry service, a uniform shop, a travel agency, and a Navy Federal Credit Union office. For more information about the Midstore, visit www.usna-store.com or www.navyonline.com.

Military Time

The fundamental difference between military time and civilian time is that military time is based on a twenty-four-hour clock instead of a twelve-hour one. The military hours from 1:00 AM to 12:00 noon translates into 0100 (pronounced "zero one hundred") hours to 1200 (twelve hundred) hours. Simple. Then, for PM times, add twelve. Thus, 1:00 PM to 12:00 midnight translates into 1300 (thirteen hundred) hours to 2400 (twenty-four hundred) hours. Other examples are shown in table 11.

Moving

The U.S. Navy or U.S. Marine Corps pay most of the moving expenses of officers, including newly commissioned ensigns and second lieutenants. A midshipman/officer arranges such a permanent change-of-duty move

Table 11. Examples of Civilian vs. Military Time

Civilian Time	Military Time	Pronunciation
1:30 AM	0130	zero one thirty
5:54 AM	0554	zero five fifty-four
1:15 PM	1315	thirteen fifteen
8:40 PM	2040	twenty forty
12:06 AM	0006	zero zero zero six

through the personnel property division, much of which is now located online (www.smartwebmove.navsup.navy.mil). For payment purposes, the move may be from either the Academy or from a permanent address (usually a hometown), or sometimes both, to the new duty station.

The Museum

The Naval Academy Museum is located in Preble Hall. It is open seven days a week. It has numerous displays and about fifty thousand items. The museum also plays a major role elsewhere on the Yard, notably John Paul Jones's crypt (see "Crypt" section in this chapter), Memorial Hall, and the various monuments. The museum acts variously as caretaker, curator of exhibits, and maintainer of property records and inventories. For more information about the museum, visit www.usna.edu/Museum.

NAPS

The Naval Academy Prep School (NAPS) is located in Newport, Rhode Island. It is called NAPS by everyone who refers to it. The school began in Newport in 1915 with thirteen enlisted sailors. It then moved to Norfolk, Virginia (1920), then to the Bainbridge Naval Training Center about forty miles north of Baltimore (1943), back to Newport (1950), back to Bainbridge (1951), and back to Newport (1975), where it remains.

No one applies directly to NAPS. The Naval Academy refers to NAPS those applicants it feels could benefit from a year there prior to Academy admission. NAPS annually enrolls about 230; the Academy subsequently enrolls about 180 NAPSters. NAPS's primary purpose is to strengthen the academics of Academy prospects from the fleet including the U.S. Marine Corps, the U.S. Naval Reserve, and certain civilian minorities and athletes seeking Academy appointments. To attend NAPS, civilians must first enlist in the U.S. Naval Reserve. There is no fee; there is no boot camp. There is, however, preliminary training upon arrival regarding the specifics of military life.

In August, NAPSters begin a ten-month program of academics and military training. To win appointments to the Academy NAPSters must complete the Academy-oriented academics successfully, generally with a C average as well as no Fs and no more than two Ds, and receive a favorable recommendation from the NAPS director.

NAPSters gaining appointments do not need separate nominations to enter the Academy; they are sworn in on I-Day with other appointees.

A midshipman stands in formation in front of his new recruits; he is a detailer during the initial training at the Naval Academy Prep School (NAPS).
Courtesy of USNA

Those failing or disenrolling from NAPS during the year may return to the fleet or return to civilian status if they went to NAPS as civilians. For more information about NAPS, visit www.naps.edu.

The Naval Institute

Formed in 1873 and headquartered in Beach Hall on Hospital Point, the private and nonprofit U.S. Naval Institute promotes knowledge of the Navy and Marine Corps. Its principal roles are book publisher (serving as the Academy's university press) and as publisher of the monthly *Proceedings* magazine. It also maintains a bookstore, book service, and research library.

In addition, the U.S. Naval Institute's eighty-five thousand members receive discounts on various books, publications, photographs, and prints. Members may participate in seminars arranged by the institute. For more information about the U.S. Naval Institute, visit www.usni.org.

News Media

Newspapers

Almost all midshipmen receive their news from online sources. They may, however, buy subscriptions for newspaper delivery to their rooms, but this has become extremely rare. The newspapers most readily available include:

> [Annapolis] Capital (www.hometownannapolis.com)
> Baltimore Sun (www.sunspot.net)
> New York Times (www.nytimes.com)
> USA Today (www.usatoday.com)
> Wall Street Journal (www.wsj.com)
> Washington Post (www.washingtonpost.com)
> Washington Times (www.washtimes.com)

Magazines

Midshipmen may subscribe to magazines for delivery by mail.

Radio

About three dozen AM and FM stations, including the midshipman-run WRNV (www.usna.edu/WRNV) serve the Annapolis area. They are based in Annapolis, Baltimore, and Washington, D.C. Upperclass midshipmen are allowed to have radios. Many midshipmen, however, listen to music either online and/or through their computers. Plebes are not allowed to listen to radios, but this policy is difficult to enforce.

Television

A number of network stations from Baltimore, Washington, and Annapolis serve the Annapolis area. The Academy does have access to cable stations, accessible by company wardroom televisions. Midshipmen may not have televisions in their rooms. Furthermore, all midshipmen computers are hooked up to the Naval Academy Data Network (NADN), a closed-circuit information network. Through this network, they can watch certain films and news programs that may be either assigned for class or allowed by their professors and/or Company Officers.

The Officers' Club

The Officers' and Faculty Club is sometimes called the O&F club. More often it's called either the Officers' Club or the O Club.

The O Club is located on the Yard near Gate 3. It has more than twenty-seven hundred dues-paying members, including some first class midshipmen. This facility is a favorite place to lunch while on the Yard. Additionally, many graduates use it for wedding receptions, special dinners, and banquets. For more information, visit www.usna.edu/MWR/club.htm.

Other Military Academies

There are four other military academies that, similar to the U.S. Naval Academy, award Bachelor of Science degrees.

The U.S. Military Academy (USMA), almost universally referred to as "West Point," is located on the Hudson River about fifty miles north of New York City in Highland Falls, New York. It was founded in 1802. Those attending are called "cadets." Enrollment is regulated by law; it has an authorized complement identical to the Naval Academy. Class designations are plebe, yearling, cow, and firstie. Graduates are commissioned as second lieutenants in the U.S. Army. For more information, visit www.usma.edu.

The U.S. Air Force Academy, located in Colorado Springs, Colorado, was founded in 1954. Those attending are called "cadets." Enrollment is regulated by law; it has an authorized complement identical to the Naval Academy. Class designations are doolie, third class, second class, and firstie. Graduates are commissioned as second lieutenants in the U.S. Air Force. For more information, visit www.usafa.af.mil.

The U.S. Coast Guard Academy, on the Thames River in New London, Connecticut, was founded in 1876. Those attending are called "cadets." Class designations are fourth class (swabs during fourth class summer), third class, second class, and first class. Total enrollment each year is about nine hundred. Graduates are commissioned as ensigns in the U.S. Coast Guard. For more information, please visit www.cga.edu.

The U.S. Merchant Marine Academy, on Long Island in King's Point, New York, was founded in 1938. Those attending are called "midshipmen." Class designations are fourth class (plebes), third class, second class, and first class. Total enrollment each year is about one thousand. Graduates are offered commissions in either the U.S. Naval Reserve (about 20 percent) or the U.S. Merchant Marines (about 80 percent). For more information, visit www.usmma.edu.

Parades

Parades at the Naval Academy are impressive. Many midshipmen spend a good deal of time drilling for them. Everyone who attends home football games should remember that the march-over from the Academy to the football stadium is not a parade, but rather something else entirely. Parades include close-order drill with rifles; march-ons are simply an organized manner of getting midshipmen from the Yard to the stadium.

Parades take place on the Worden Field parade ground. They are held on special occasions and periodically throughout the year, usually in late September and October (sometimes running into November) and in April. A few plebe parades occur during Plebe Summer. In addition, a number of parades are held during Commissioning Week, including the Dedication Parade and the Color Parade.

Parents Organizations

While U.S. Naval Academy's parents organizations have existed for many years, the computer and Internet have really afforded these groups the opportunity to become much more involved, active, accurate, and connected. The organizations are by and large fantastic. They are overwhelmingly supportive, both locally and nationwide, and come in all different sizes. Each has its own mission. Some are sponsored by the Academy itself, others are not. An official Academy sponsorship does not necessarily indicate a "better" or "worse" group. Any favorite Internet search engine will likely yield a number of groups targeted toward the things that interest parents, but the one thing connecting them all is a passion for the well-being of their children enrolled at the Naval Academy.

Parents organization Web sites can serve as an invaluable complement to the contents of this book. Many sites allow parents to communicate with each other in chat-room environments. Some sites keep archives and files on key topics, thus allowing curious parents (usually new Academy parents) the opportunity to see what other parents have previously shared regarding similar topics. Some groups pray together. Others advise nervous parents how to act and what to bring to all occasions from I-Day to Commissioning Week.

To summarize, if you are a parent of a soon-to-be midshipman or are the parent of a current midshipman, I strongly encourage you to become involved in one or more of these parents groups. In the long run, you will be better prepared to assist your child in his or her Academy experience, something many parents long for but only a percentage fulfill. Parents may also may make a few new friends in the process. Searching of Web sites can begin with the following:

http://usna.com/Communities/parents/parents/htm
www.usna.org
www.usna-net.org/clublinks.html

Parents Weekends

There are two parents weekends: Plebe Parents Weekend and First Class Parents Weekend. Plebe Parents Weekend occurs in mid-August at the end of Plebe Summer and is considered by many parents to be the most important event for parents during their midshipman's entire four years. In most cases it will provide the first opportunity for parents to see their new midshipman since I-Day and vice versa. Be there! Get a hotel, motel, or B&B room. Stay for the duration. Do whatever your plebe wants to do. And remain positive, supportive, and upbeat.

First Class Parents Weekend usually occurs in early September. Perhaps less important than Plebe Parents Weekend, it nevertheless provides an important opportunity for parents to see their son or daughter in the Academy environment as he or she begins the final year. First Class Parents Weekend also affords parents the opportunity to attend classes with their midshipman, something many parents look forward to and enjoy.

Parking

On the Yard

Parking is very tight on the Yard. The Department of Defense (DOD) police enforce parking regulations as vigorously as the Maryland police do in Annapolis. Also, remember that the Naval Academy is a federal facility. Parking violations, as well as moving violations, especially speeding, find resolution in a federal magistrate system. Parking violations carry stiff fines. When visiting the Yard, park only in lots or where the surface or curbs are unpainted. If the curb is painted, you cannot park there. Period.

In Annapolis

In Annapolis, parking is available in six public-access facilities. On-street parking, in both metered and nonmetered areas, is limited to two hours and is usually very difficult to find. Parking is usually available at the

Navy-Marine Corps Memorial Stadium, with shuttle service to the Academy and downtown.

Annapolis is a small, quaint town. The Academy is likewise a fairly small, quaint complex. It is best to equate this quaintness, therefore, with very limited parking. Parking has a profound ability to cause headaches. Just be prepared and wear good walking shoes. There is even a saying around town, "Come to Annapolis and take home a souvenir: get a parking ticket."

Phones

See "Telephones" section in this chapter.

Publications

Midshipmen are responsible for producing the following publications:

> *The Lucky Bag* (yearbook)
> *Reef Points* (an annual for plebes)
> *The Labyrinth* (the Academy's literary magazine)

In addition, other Academy publications include:

> *The Trident* (a weekly tabloid newspaper published by the public affairs office); available online at www.dcmilitary.com/navy/trident
> *Shipmate* (a monthly alumni magazine published by the U.S. Naval Academy Alumni Association)
> *Naval History* (a quarterly journal published by the U.S. Naval Institute)
> *Proceedings* (a monthly magazine about Navy and Marine Corps matters, with occasional articles about the Academy, published by the U.S. Naval Institute)

The Naval Academy's public affairs office can suggest a number of ways—published and electronic—for learning more about Yard events that affect midshipmen. For more information, visit www.usna.edu/PAO.

Sponsors

During Plebe Summer, under what is dubbed the plebe sponsor program, every midshipman who desires is linked with a family inside a twenty-two-mile radius of the Academy. When a family knows an incoming midshipman, the link can be easily prearranged.

These volunteer families, called sponsors, serve as homes away from homes—not only for plebes but for midshipmen during their entire Academy careers. Sponsors frequently become key connections with the world beyond the wall and frequently become friends for life. All midshipmen should take full advantage of this remarkable opportunity.

Synagogue

See "Worship" section in this chapter.

Tailgating

Tailgating has long been a tradition at football games, and a growing one at other athletic events. At home football games, the entire parking area surrounding the stadium is available—and used for—tailgating. Spreads range from the bare minimum to the unbelievably elaborate (for example, with china and crystal). Some are unbelievable!

Midshipmen are not allowed to attend a tailgating party prior to a football game or at halftime, but can drop by a tailgating party after the game. Be sure to have what they like, but remember to abide by Academy rules and Maryland laws relating to alcohol. The Academy is increasingly strict regarding alcohol and a friendly beer or two to a midshipman may get that midshipman into a world of trouble. Review the "Drugs and Alcohol" section in this chapter.

Take-Out

Some Annapolis eateries deliver to midshipmen at the Academy. But there's a hitch. Drivers of telephoned orders, for example, pizza or Chinese food, are directed to either gate zero (the pedestrian-only gate behind Halsey Field House) or Gate 1. Midshipmen must meet and pay the driver for the order at the gate.

Tecumseh

Tecumseh is actually the bronze statue of Tamanend, a peaceful Delaware chief. Many years ago, midshipmen nicknamed the statue

Each week prior to home football games, plebes paint the Tecumseh statue to show Brigade spirit; here he is wearing patriotic garb.
Courtesy of USNA

"Tecumseh" after the war-loving Shawnee chief. The statue, in front of Bancroft Hall, keeps watch over T-Court. Tecumseh is frequently called the "God of 2.0"; some midshipmen toss pennies at Tecumseh en route to their exams for good luck, trying to get the pennies in his quiver (which, by the way, is solid). Tecumseh is painted by plebes, usually during the week prior to each home football game and prior to Commissioning Week. The paint is water soluble and the practice supposedly shows Brigade spirit.

Telephones

Amid much grumbling and consternation by many alumni and some Academy administration officials, every room in Bancroft Hall now has its own phone. The phone numbers coordinate to the room numbers. For example, the Xs in 1-443-321-XXXX designate the four-digit room number.

The decision to include phones in each room was made for many reasons. As part of the incredible eleven-year, $251 million Bancroft Hall renovations, each room was wired with phone lines for Internet use. Furthermore, the Academy had—for many years prior—fought a losing battle against the midshipmen having their own mobile phones in their rooms. Of course, the reception for mobile phones inside an enormous stone building such as Bancroft Hall was poor at best. On any given night many midshipmen could be seen hanging out of their windows or standing outside the building in all kinds of weather chatting away on their mobile phones.

The presence of telephones in the rooms has dramatically altered the way parents can communicate with their midshipman. In short, if a parent wants to get in touch with his or her mid, call or e-mail. Do not call the Company Officer. Do not call the Battalion Officer. Do not call the Commandant. Do not call the Superintendent. Any calls to these individuals (with the exception of an emergency) will result in the midshipman receiving very unwanted attention, regardless of how good the parent's original intentions were.

There are other telephone numbers that can and should be used appropriately as needed. The main office in Bancroft Hall is manned twenty-four hours a day. Its numbers are:

410-293-5001
410-293-5002
410-293-5003

For a list of other important phone numbers that the public affairs office publishes, visit www.usna.edu/PAO/phone.htm.

Tickets

The Naval Academy Athletic Association (NAAA) sells tickets to all Navy sporting events. Football tickets are available for individual games or for the full home-game season. A low-cost membership in NAAA provides certain benefits, including savings on season tickets. Season tickets generally offer better seat location, per-ticket savings, and savings on stadium parking. For more information regarding sporting event tickets, visit www.navysports.com/info/tickets or call 1-800-US4-NAVY.

There also exist two other ticket offices at the Academy, one in Bancroft Hall and one across the Severn River at the naval station. The Bancroft Hall office sells discounted tickets to recreational activities to midshipmen, including Disney World, Epcot Center, and Busch Gardens. The office sells discounted tickets to local movie theaters and lift tickets to nearby ski resorts. It also sells tickets to all music- and cultural-related events that take place on the Yard, including band concerts (Dave Matthews, Faith Hill, Vince Gill, and the Goo Goo Dolls, to name a few), comedian and magic shows (for example, Bill Cosby and Penn & Teller), the Distinguished Artist Series (international ballet troupes, international operas and symphonies), the Masqueraders' fall drama, and the Glee Club's winter musical. Tickets for most of these types of events can be purchased at www.tickets.com. However, the Distinguished Artist Series is a subscriber series for which there is currently a waiting list. For more information on the Distinguished Artist Series, visit www.usna.edu/Music/distartseries.html. All tickets (including Distinguished Artist Series) may be purchased by calling the Bancroft Hall ticket office at 410-293-8497. The ticket office at the naval station sells all recreational tickets except for any music- or cultural-related tickets.

Tobacco

Use of tobacco is discouraged and, in most places in Bancroft Hall, forbidden. Midshipmen are allowed to smoke, but only in very few, very specifically designated smoking areas. Furthermore, they are not allowed to chew or dip tobacco in class.

Tours (Public, Not Marching)

Guided tours of the Naval Academy are handled by the guide service operated out of the Armel-Leftwich Visitor Center; the service gives about 100,000 tours a year. These tours are limited to the Academy and the Yard. For more information on guided tours, visit www.navyonline.com or call 410-263-6933.

Commercial guide companies based in Annapolis also give tours of the Annapolis historic area; some of these tours include parts of the Academy as well. For more information about Annapolis tours, visit www.annapolis-tours.com.

Transportation

When in Annapolis, there are many options for going places without driving your own car. Annapolis has several cab and car rental services. A commuter bus connects to the New Carrollton Metro, which can be boarded for the subway ride to the Washington, D.C., area. The metro is easy and inexpensive for getting around the city. Limousines and shuttle vans provide services from various points in Annapolis to almost anywhere, including the major nearby airports.

Options for getting to Annapolis without a car include taking buses from Washington, D.C., or Baltimore. Cabs are plentiful. Airport limousines and shuttle vans provide transportation from all surrounding airports, even as far away as Philadelphia.

Upperclass midshipmen may rent cars if they meet a given company's stipulated age for rental. Such ages vary from company to company.

The amount of information online regarding travel and transportation is exhausting. You may arrange travel to and from Annapolis in much the same way you would to any other city for a vacation. That said, perhaps the below Web sites will help you in making your plans.

Baltimore-Washington International Airport: www.bwiairport.com

Dulles International Airport: www.metwashairports.com/Dulles

Washington National (Reagan) Airport: www.metwashairports.com/National/Index.html

Maryland Transit Authority: www.mtamaryland.com/index.cfm

AMTRAK: www.amtrak.com

Washington Metropolitan Area Transit Authority: www.wmata.com/default.cfm

Travel

As members of the military, midshipmen may receive considerable savings from commercial airlines and car rental companies. Such companies require that as a condition of such savings, midshipmen show their military identification on request.

A travel service is in operation adjacent to Bancroft Hall's third wing basement: Omega World Travel. For more information, visit www.owt.net/ or call 888-314-6956 (toll-free) or 410-280-9755.

In addition, midshipmen may travel "space-available" on Air Mobility Command (AMC) flights between domestic and foreign military facilities. A few AMC terminals close to Annapolis are Andrews Air Force Base (east of Washington, D.C.), Dover Air Force Base (Dover, Delaware), and the AMC terminal at Baltimore-Washington International

(BWI) Airport. Reliability for AMC flights is iffy at best, rendering use of AMC flights questionable for midshipmen with strict travel deadlines. The Midshipmen Store has guide books that provide current information about flying space-available on AMC flights. Also, many Web sites exist with AMC information, but most of those are restricted to military access.

Visiting

See "Parents Weekends" and "Tours" sections in this chapter.

Weddings

Many Naval Academy graduates want to get married in the chapel. These weddings are common—often back-to-back—during Commissioning Week and thereafter. As many as thirty have occurred in the week immediately following Commissioning Week, with up to eight a day. During such days, and prescribed Saturdays throughout the year, the chapel is literally a wedding factory.

Arrangements should begin at least a year in advance. The chaplain's office offers premarriage counseling and also arranges all coordination. There is a handbook containing wedding information and an application for a chapel ceremony. For more information regarding Academy weddings, contact the wedding coordinator at 410-293-1105.

Worship

Attendance at church is encouraged but not required. Midshipmen may attend Catholic and Protestant services on Sunday at the main chapel, or Jewish services on Friday evenings at the All Faiths Chapel in Mitscher Hall. The new Commodore Uriah P. Levy Center, which will contain the Jewish Chapel and an ethics, leadership, and fellowship center, is scheduled for completion in summer 2004. In addition, Catholic masses and Protestant devotionals and communions are held variously in Mitscher Hall and in St. Andrew's Chapel (in the main chapel's lower level). Islamic services are held on Fridays; Buddhist services are held on Tuesdays. Other services available include Hindu, Native American, and Latter Day Saints. In short, any faith or desire to worship is accommodated by the Academy chaplain's center. Midshipmen also may attend churches and synagogues in Annapolis. The Academy's chaplains and rabbis offer counseling and denominational instruction.

The U.S. Naval Academy Chapel in springtime.
Courtesy of USNA

The Year

Schedules for the year are commonplace at the Academy. However, they seldom find their way to parents. Thanks to the Internet, however, parents may access schedules easily. For general information regarding schedules and calendars, visit www.usna.edu/PAO/calendars.htm. For more specific scheduling information, parents, family members, and friends should contact the midshipman, Bancroft Hall's main office, or the public affairs office.

Table 12 shows some routine scheduling highlights.

Table 12. Routine Midshipman Schedule for the Year

Day	Comments
Late August	Summer leave ends; first semester begins
Labor Day	Holiday
Columbus Day	Holiday
Veterans Day	Holiday
Thanksgiving	Leave from last obligation on the Wednesday before Thanksgiving until dinnertime the Sunday following (four days)
Early December	Army-Navy football game
Mid-December	Exams begin (ten days); midshipmen may begin Christmas leave following their last exam; leave lasts two to three weeks
Early January	Christmas leave ends; second semester begins
Martin Luther King Day	Holiday
President's Day	Holiday
Early March	Spring vacation begins (ten days or one week and two weekends)
Early May	Exams begin (about one week)
May	Commissioning Week; begins on a Saturday with Ring Dance; ends with graduation the following Friday
After Commissioning Week	Summer leave and summer training begin
Late June, early July	Induction of the new plebe class

—8—

Midspeak

A Dictionary of the U.S. Naval Academy Language

Ward Carroll, a naval flight officer, former U.S. Naval Academy instructor, and author, wrote in *Punk's War* (Annapolis, Md.: Naval Institute Press, 2001) that naval aviation yields an "axiom-rich lexicon." That is true. So does the U.S. Navy in general. So does the military as a whole, with each subset, branch, and community inventing, cultivating, and perpetuating its own specific language. The various lexicons combine acronyms, slang, abbreviations, and colloquialisms to form unique tongues. The Naval Academy is no different.

Some words used at the Academy are heard throughout the Navy, some throughout all the U.S. military organizations. Like all languages, the Naval Academy's language—Midspeak—lives; it is ever changing.

The following dictionary of terms is as complete and accurate as possible. Some alumni and former military personnel may not find words here that they once used. Some may be happy to learn that a portion of their generation of words are still around. Most words, terms, and phrases appear here unfettered and without editorialization; the definitions are primarily those of the midshipmen and Academy personnel who speak the language. This presentation is the result of years of research, modifications, and recommendations by current and past midshipmen, faculty, administration officials, and staff. In short, this is Midspeak as it exists today. It is presented here to aid understanding of the vernacular of the Yard and those who inhabit it.

academic accountability Requirement that midshipmen attend all their classes (and be on time) unless they have valid excuses; unexcused absences and/or tardies lead to conduct action.

academic adviser Teacher within a midshipman's major assigned to him or her for academic guidance and course selection; each plebe is assigned an adviser during Plebe Summer; after selecting a major in the spring of plebe year, he or she is assigned a new adviser for the next three years from the department of his or her major.

academically deficient A term decreasing in use, giving way to the more prevalent unsat; a midshipman with a cumulative quality point rating (CQPR) below 2.0 is academically deficient and must undertake corrective study measures as outlined by his or her Company Officer. See also *unsat.*

Academic Board Academic discipline board that convenes at the end of each semester to review poor academic performance and to determine separation or retention (technically, each midshipman attending such a board has already been separated and the board's job is to determine whether the midshipman shall be readmitted); its members are the Superintendent, the Commandant, the Dean, and the four division directors, with the director of admissions serving as secretary; called "Ac Board" by midshipmen.

academic help Academic assistance; midshipmen have a variety of formal options for academic assistance including (1) voluntary or mandatory extra instruction (EI) from any instructor during the class day or at night, and (2) help through the Academic Center, the Writing Center, math lab, and midshipmen tutors.

academic probation Midshipmen may find themselves on academic probation for a variety of reasons—generally if they have low cumulative quality point rating (CQPRs); in the words of an official statement: "The purpose of academic probation is to warn midshipmen their [academic] performance is below the required standards and significant improvement will be required to justify further retention at the Naval Academy"; midshipmen remove themselves from probation by clearing their academic deficiencies.

academic tracking sheet Form, or study log, that most unsat midshipmen must fill out to show how they have spent their study hours; sometimes referred to as "weekly honor violations."

Ac Board Pronounced "ack board." See *Academic Board.*

accreditation The U.S. Naval Academy is accredited by the Middle States Association of Colleges and Secondary Schools; where such accreditation is available, its majors are also accredited by appropriate discipline groups.

ac year   Pronounced "ack year." Short for academic year; the period between August and early May when midshipmen attend academic classes.

ADEO   Alcohol and drug education officer; a midshipman in each company who deals with alcohol- and drug-related affairs.

Advisory Board   Board, lower than the Academic Board, that meets at the end of each semester with midshipmen regarding academic difficulties and decides such things as whether they will repeat a failed course, change a major, or attend summer school.

aero   Short for aeronautical engineering.

affirmative   Military-wide term for "yes." See *negative.*

airdale   Military-wide nickname for a pilot or for enlisted personnel in the various aviation communities; used most frequently by sailors.

Air Force Academy   The U.S. Air Force Academy in Colorado Springs, Colorado; its class designations—in order—are doolie, third class, second class, and firstie. See also *West Point.*

Air Force Week   Week preceding the Navy–Air Force football game, featuring activities and pranks designed to promote Brigade spirit; only observed during certain years, the pranks are conducted on a smaller, gentler scale, almost as a warm-up for Army Week.

alcohol   The law is twenty-one in Maryland; on the Yard, alcohol may be consumed legally and within Academy regulations only when and where approved by the Commandant (usually, on stipulated occasions, in Dahlgren, Sailing Center, Hubbard Hall, Alumni Hall, and at the O Club); the misuse of alcohol by midshipmen is a severely fryable offense.

all calls   Requirement, as punishment, that a plebe perform chow calls more frequently than usual—for instance, every minute for ten minutes before breakfast and lunch, instead of just ten minutes and five minutes before.

alpha code   Identifying six-digit number given to every midshipman on I-Day, and used throughout one's Naval Academy career on everything from forms to gear; it is as important as a social security number; the first two digits indicate the year of graduation.

alpha inspection   Very formal room inspection (white glove). See *inspections.*

AMCMO   Acronym for assistant midshipman in charge of main office, a second class billet.

amnesty   See *presidential pardon.*

AMOOW   Acronym for assistant midshipman officer of the watch, a company commander billet in main office under the OOW.

anchor   (1) Midshipman with the lowest order of merit in the class, frequently called the "anchorman" (the firstie who graduates last in the class receives a dollar from each classmate—and among those close, competition is often keen); the lowest-rated anything (individual or unit). (2) Central, or crossing, point of the "T" in King Hall—where prior to meals the bell is rung, announcements are given, the prayer is said, and determined declarations are made to beat the next beleaguered athletic opponent.

anchorman   See *anchor.*

another great Navy day   Navy-wide phrase of pretended, or mock, exuberance.

Army Week   Week preceding the Army-Navy football game, featuring activities and pranks designed to promote Brigade spirit. See also *Air Force Week.*

article   Plebe rate; generally, the requirement that a plebe read one news article regarding world (international) events, one article regarding national events, and one sports-page article, all usually from their chosen Internet news source; they must be able to converse at least three minutes about each.

ASAP   Military-wide acronym for as soon as possible.

assassination   Motivational stunt pulled by plebes in King Hall in which a plebe sneaks under a table and slathers condiments (peanut butter, catsup, chocolate sauce, etc) on an upperclass's shoe(s), then escapes without being caught; tradition has it that if the plebe makes it up to his or her room without being caught by the upperclass, he or she is home free; if caught, however, the plebe's life will certainly become unpleasant. See also *wildman* and *Princess Leia.*

ASTB   Acronym for Aviation Selection Test Battery, a two and a half hour, five-part test for prospective aviators; it has a math/verbal section similar to the Scholastic Aptitude Test (SAT), as well as parts on mechanical comprehension, spatial perception, aviation and nautical information, and aviation interest; offered in second class year and sometimes during third class summer; those failing to achieve minimum requirements are ineligible for flight assignments.

attrition   For all reasons (that is, not just academic reasons), about 25 percent of those enrolled fail to graduate—giving the Naval Academy a

75 percent graduation (or retention) rate; nationally, for all colleges, the four-year graduation rate is less than 50 percent.

attrition classes   Those classes with traditionally high failure rates, which thereby augment the Academy's attrition rate—notably chemistry for plebes, physics for youngsters, and electrical engineering (double E) for second class.

augmentation   Navy-wide term for moving from the reserve to the regular service. When used as a verb, means to augment up.

aweigh   As in "anchor's aweigh"; when the anchor is free of the bottom, meaning the ship is under way.

AWOL   Military-wide acronym for absent without leave, a severely fryable offense. See also *UA*.

backseater   Nickname for a naval flight officer. See *NFO*.

balls   Military-wide reference to midnight because in military time, midnight is represented by four zeros (empty balls); the "balls to four watch" is the midnight until 4:00 AM watch.

banana stickers   Dole and Chiquita stickers placed inside midshipmen covers; they represent alleged sexual activity and rendezvous on Academy grounds and/or within Bancroft Hall itself.

Bancroft   Bancroft Hall; home sweet home; usually called "the Hall"; never called "Mother B."

barn   One of a few large rooms in Bancroft Hall containing four or more roommates; some are even called "suites."

basic response   See *responses*.

The Basic School   Training facility located in Quantico, Virginia; where U.S. Marine Corps second lieutenants go for training after graduation; frequently called TBS.

basket leave   Thirty days of leave given to all midshipmen upon graduation; they must use it within ninety days of graduation, or not at all.

battalion   Unit of organization within the Brigade; each regiment has three battalions; each battalion is composed of companies.

Batt-O   Short for Battalion Officer, who works in one of the battalion offices, which are sometimes referred to as the "BOOW shack"; some claim that the Batt-O works in a "batt cave"; the Batt-O is above the Company Officer and below the Deputy Commandant; each battalion office is overseen by the BOOW, a firstie, and an ABOOW, a second class.

beat army   A drink only consumed in King Hall usually during Army Week by plebes as a show of motivation; beat armys are made by upperclass who combine anything on a given table in King Hall, for example, milk, juice, mayonnaise, chocolate syrup, salad dressing, peanut butter, Tabasco, etc.; following consumption, the plebe frequently vomits, usually to cheers of applause from adjoining tables.

"Beat Army, sir!"   One of two cries shouted by plebes when they square corners; the other is "Go Navy, sir!"; without the "sir," it is always yelled after the singing of "Navy Blue and Gold."

bed check   Usually on weekends, an after-hours check to determine the presence of midshipmen in their rooms.

bell   (1) Electronic bell that rings in Bancroft Hall for reveille and classes. (2) Bell at the central point (the anchor) of King Hall rung prior to meals. (3) Bell in T-Court rung at the conclusion of each sports season by each varsity athlete who contributed to a victory over Army.

bet   Wager made between plebes and upperclass on football games; the stakes are never money, but always require plebes to bet on Navy, usually a losing bet.

BGMJS   Acronym for blue and gold monogrammed jogging suit. According to midshipmen, the very cheesy warm-ups worn by midshipmen with one's name and class monogrammed on the jacket; cheesy or not, these are considered uniforms and allow the midshipmen opportunities to *not* have to wear an actual—usually more constrictive—uniform.

bilge   When used as a verb, means to undercut, stab in the back, make another look bad ("Don't bilge your classmate"). Also used as a noun, meaning one who bilges another; bilging is officially outlawed during Plebe Summer in an attempt to promote covering a shipmate's actions.

bilger's gate   Pedestrian gates on either side of Gate 3; tradition has it that many years ago when a midshipman separated, he left the Academy through one of these gates; because of this superstition, no midshipman will walk through these gates until he or she has graduated.

Bill's anatomy   Testicles of the bronze statue of Bill the Goat; this part of the statue is the only shiny part, the result of plebes who have lost bets to their upperclass and must, under cover of darkness, shine away. See also *ride the goat.*

Bill the Goat and his handlers attend a Navy football game.
Courtesy of USNA

Bill the Goat   U.S. Naval Academy mascot off and on since 1893, when a
   goat named "El Cid" appeared at an Army-Navy football game in
   which Navy prevailed 6-4; in the subsequent decade a dog, two cats,
   and a carrier pigeon served briefly as mascots, but Bill has been the
   official mascot since 1904; he is trotted out for football games and
   pep rallies; also a bronze statue of the mascot just inside Gate 1 in
   front of Lejune Hall. See also *ride the goat* and *Bill's anatomy*.

billet   Navy-wide term for a position, job, designation, duty assignment,
   slot, or space ("He got an air billet," "My company billet is . . . ," or
   "They ran out of billets").

birth control glasses (BCGs)   See *geekers*.

birthday ball   Dance celebrating the November 10 birthday of the U.S.
   Marine Corps; attended by Marine Corps officers and by prior-
   enlisted Marines who are currently midshipmen, plus their wives or
   dates.

birthday party   What periodically happens to someone who is celebrating
   an actual birthday, sometimes in King Hall, sometimes in company
   areas; an excuse to give "special" attention to someone by making his
   or her life a little more difficult (shaving cream in face, condiments
   on head, water dumped on head, etc.). See also *wildman*.

black flag   When the heat index (a combination of humidity and temperature) is too high for any outdoor physical activity during Plebe Summer; in short, the answer to plebe prayers.

Black N   Symbol of extreme conduct and/or honor infraction(s). See Conduct section in the Military chapter (Chapter 3).

blackshoe   Navy-wide nickname for a surface warfare officer or enlisted personnel who work on ships; frequently referred to as a "shoe."

blocks   Usually refers to the three segments of summer training, called first, second, and third blocks; each is about a month long. For more specifics, see the Military chapter (Chapter 3).

blood pins   Any pin awarded for military achievement, such as airborne or scuba; the phrase comes from the Navy-wide rite of smacking such pins (aviator wings, SEAL Trident, etc.), with their two or three prongs in back, into the wearer's chest, usually drawing blood; now considered hazing throughout the Navy, it is forbidden and severely prosecuted.

blow off   Used as a verb, meaning to pay insufficient attention to, as in "He blew her off" or "Of course he flunked Chem. He blew it off all year."

blue and gold   (1) Short for "Navy Blue and Gold," the U.S. Naval Academy alma mater. (2) The Academy's official colors.

Blue and Gold Officer (BGO)   Any of many U.S. Naval Academy alumni and friends throughout the country who provide information to prospective midshipmen and assist them in the admissions process.

The Bluejackets' Manual   Basic handbook of information for sailors since 1902.

blue magnet   Nickname for the bedspread on every midshipman's bed; "blue" because of the color, "magnet" because of the seductive power it has over its owner. See also *rack monster.*

blue rim   Standard-issue midshipman T-shirt; the top half of reg PE gear.

board   Hearing or any formal session with any of various boards, for example, academic, advisory, conduct, performance.

boards   Any of the bulletin boards in a company area; the responsibility of decorating these boards with artwork and motivational materials falls on the plebes; deadlines are usually set for such creativity, and if such deadlines are not met, loss of liberty is usually the punishment; real aggravations for any plebe with any artistic ability.

boats   Nickname for a required engineering/naval architecture course; advanced students and those majoring in the area take the course called "ships."

boat school   Probably the most common of many nicknames for the U.S. Naval Academy; others include Camp Tecumseh, Canoe U, Chesapeake University of Naval Technology, and the Severn River Institute for High School Over-Achievers.

BOHICA   Military-wide acronym used frequently by midshipmen, stands for "Bend over, here it comes again."

bone   A bad deal ("He got the bone"); some suggest that the yin and yang of the Academy is the hook and the bone. Also used as a verb ("That prof boned us with that test").

bonk   Used as a verb, a term borrowed from extreme sports (mountain/rock climbing, triathlons, marathons, etc.) essentially describing physical body shut down evidenced (medically) by a drop in blood pressure and profound decrease in performance ("He bonked"). See *hit the wall.*

boondocker   Navy standard-issue low boot, higher than an oxford but not a full boot; primarily worn by enlisted personnel and not officers.

BOOW   Acronym for battalion officer of the watch, who is a firstie.

A plebe marching with his rifle gives a good illustration of a brace.
Courtesy of USNA

brace up   Used as a verb, instructing plebes to assume an exaggerated position of attention while producing as many chins as possible with the chin tucked into the neck cavity, eyes straight ahead; bracing—the noun form—is a required plebe rite exhibiting motivation and submission; now prohibited in King Hall; "get a brace" is also used.

brag sheet   Paper prepared by a midshipman about himself or herself, setting down the midshipman's achievements for consideration in determining performance rating.

brain-dump   Used as a verb, meaning to purge the mind; to empty it of every pertinent thing following the need to know it ("Now that the year is over, I'm brain-dumping chemistry"); based on the assumption that the brain can only hold a finite amount of information, brain dumping is critical to allow room for other items of interest and knowledge.

brassard   Band of cloth worn around the upper sleeve, indicating a temporary duty assignment (such as watch or usher); also called a "duty cuff" and (simply) "armband."

bravo zulu (BZ)   From the phonetic alphabet, a Navy-wide term meaning well done ("a BZ—or bravo zulu—performance").

brick   A physical brick that plebes give their company's upperclass who had the weekend's most unfortunate-looking date; in single file, plebes shuffle rhythmically through their company area chanting, "The brick. The brick. Who gets the brick?"; the line stops outside the winner's door and the leader awards the brick; gladly given to the most disliked upperclass, regardless of what his or her date looked like.

Brigade   Collective noun for all the midshipmen as a group: the Brigade of Midshipmen. See *regiment, battalion, company, platoon,* and *squad.*

brownshoe   Navy-wide nickname for an aviator (pilot or NFO) or for enlisted personnel working in any of the various aviation communities. See *airdale.*

B.S.   (1) The degree (Bachelor of Science) granted to all graduating midshipmen, even bull majors (some say nothing could be better than to have a B.S. in, for instance, English). (2) Short for the obvious vulgarism meaning baloney or something less than the genuine article ("a bunch of B.S.").

BSA   Acronym for Brigade support activity (such as the drum and bugle corps, the cheerleaders, the cannoneers, and the silent drill team), a variety of ECA.

bubblehead   Navy-wide nickname for a submariner.

BUD/S   Acronym for basic underwater demolition/SEAL school, the SEAL basic training center in Coronado, California. See also *mini-BUD/S*.

bulkhead   Navy-wide term for any wall.

bull major   Slang for any of the group III humanities majors (English, history, economics, and political science), or any midshipman pursuing such a major ("She's a bull major"); considered derogatory by administration officials but used continuously by both midshipmen and faculty alike, especially in the particular bull major departments.

bust   When used as a noun, means a mistake; the condition of being wrong ("My bust" means, "My problem, my mistake, I was wrong"). When used as a verb, means (1) to catch someone (or to be caught) doing something one shouldn't ("He got busted for coming in late"); (2) Navy-wide term meaning to lose one (or more) pay grades ("His punishment for being caught stealing was to be busted down to an E4 from an E5").

butter bar   Slang term decreasing in use for the gold stripe on an ensign's uniform.

BWI   Baltimore/Washington International Airport; very busy during holidays.

BZ   See *bravo zulu*.

cables   Level of electrical engineering taken by group I majors; group II and group III majors take "wires"; the logic is appropriate: cables, which are very complicated, are comprised of wires.

cadet   Name of midshipman counterparts at the U.S. Air Force Academy and at West Point. See also *plebe*.

cake-eater   An officer; a term usually used by enlisted personnel; derogatory term insinuating that all officers do is sit around and eat cake. See also *SWOnut* and *ring knocker*.

calc   Short for calculus, one of two banes for many plebes. See also *chem*.

Camp Tecumseh   A now infrequently used nickname for the U.S. Naval Academy, specifically for Plebe Summer; based on the assumption (true or not) that things are now not very physically strenuous, akin to a child's summer camp.

cannonball run   A cannonball is a King Hall creation that is essentially a hard, dough-covered apple; a cannonball run is a motivational stunt pulled by plebes in which a plebe attempts to eat all twelve cannon-balls at a given table, including a bowl of "hard sauce" (essentially whipped sugar) without vomiting; a successful attempt would likely yield wonderful things for the plebe and his or her classmates; often tried; very rarely successfully completed.

Canoe U Nickname for the U.S. Naval Academy. See also *boat school*.

car Freedom (for some); only firsties may park them on the Yard and only second class may park them near the Yard; youngsters and plebes may not operate them at all.

career path (1) Midshipman's path to this point in his or her career. (2) Path projected (in terms of training and duty assignments) from this point. See also *pipeline*.

career starter loan See *second class loan*.

care package A box, usually from a sweetheart or home, that usually contains food.

carrier landings Running slides on the water-covered floors of Bancroft Hall; illegal but still performed; sometimes sanctioned on a long piece of plastic soaked by hoses on Hospital Point.

carry-on Privilege conferred on a plebe to act normally; temporary free-dom from plebe rites and obligations ("He gave us carry-on at tables"). Also used as a verb, meaning to continue normal behavior or to resume one's previous activity following an interruption; for exam-ple, when junior or subordinate people come to attention upon a sen-ior officer's entry into a room, the senior officer then tells everyone to "carry on."

cat-V Pronounced "cat-five." Short for category V of the height and weight standards; an overweight and/or fat person.

CBDR Acronym for constant bearing, decreasing range; a collision course; used only by those who drive ships or those who want to.

CDO Acronym for company duty officer, a first class who is head of a duty section in his or her company.

cell phones What most plebes get right after the Herndon (Plebe Recognition Ceremony), because they can. See also *telephone*.

CF Acronym for Charlie Foxtrot, which throughout the military stands for "cluster f°°°"; a complete mess.

chain Short for chain of command.

chain of command (1) Navy-wide term meaning administrative and operational channels; the superior-to-subordinate succession for commands; the subordinate-to-superior succession for requests. (2) The midshipman hierarchy (from squad leader to the Brigade commander) or the military hierarchy (from Company Officer to the Superintendent—and beyond); common phrases are "Use the chain of command" and "Don't jump the chain."

check six Military-wide aviation phrase, short for "Check your six o'clock," that is, "Check what's behind you"; in a crowd "I've got your six" is used, meaning "I'm following right behind you."

chem Short for chemistry, one of two banes of many plebes. See also *calc*.

chest candy Slang for breast insignia, awards, ribbons, or any extra ornaments on uniforms. See also *flare* and *Joe pins*.

chit Written permission or excusal; examples are chits for late lights (for plebes), for special liberty, or for excusing midshipmen from obligations such as classes or athletics because of injury or illness.

chitsurfer One who goes from one excuse to another; one who seldom contributes to anything requiring teamwork and always makes excuses for reasons he or she cannot participate; chitsurfers are not well liked.

choke To clutch or to tense up, and thereby (usually) to blow it.

choker whites Formal summer uniform worn in most cases during the day; the nighttime version, the equivalent of a civilian tuxedo (or dinner jacket), is dinner dress whites. See also *uniforms*.

chopping Manner in which plebes must move in Bancroft Hall's halls and stairways; plebes chop by taking short, double-time steps (about 160 steps per minute); chopping also consists of (1) moving along the center of all passageways and on the outside bulkheads of all ladders, (2) squaring all corners, and (3) sounding off with motivational phrases such as "Go Navy, sir!" and "Beat Army, sir!"; generally hated by all plebes as, perhaps, it is intended.

chow calls Plebe rates; ten minutes and five minutes before breakfast and lunch if formations are inside; twelve minutes and seven minutes before those meals if formations are outside; plebes quickly recite (1) where the formation is (inside or outside), (2) the uniform for the formation, (3) the menu for the meal, (4) the midshipman and officer on duty for the day, (5) the week's professional topic, and (6) the day's major events on the Yard; abhorred by all plebes; abhorred by upperclass who like peace and quiet; used as excuses for Joes to flame on plebes. See also *all calls*.

civilian   (1) Day on which a midshipman has no classes; see *youngster.* (2) Person with no military affiliation.

civvies   (1) Civilian clothes. (2) Civilian clothes privileges, that is, the right to come and go at the Academy in civilian clothes; civvies generally are enjoyed by all firsties and second class going on, during, and returning from liberty or leave.

class crest   Designed for each class during plebe year by a committee of midshipmen from that class; it appears on various wearing apparel, most notably on the class ring, but also on jewelry available for purchase at the end of plebe year such as pins, necklace ornaments, cuff links, and tie-tacks.

class day   It contains six 50-minute periods—four in the morning and two after lunch—Monday through Friday; there are no Saturday classes; in a few exceptional cases, a seventh period is used in the afternoon for three-period labs; at night, Sunday through Friday, the hours from 7:30 to 11:00 PM are reserved for study.

classes   U.S. Naval Academy classes, in order, are fourth class (see *plebe*), the counterpart of a civilian college freshman; third class (see *youngster*), a sophomore; second class (see *second class*), a junior; and first class (see *firstie*), a senior. See also *Air Force Academy* and *West Point.*

classmate loyalty   Concept or practice of looking out for one's own; sometimes generates conflicts with the honor concept.

class pictures   Formal in-uniform color photographs taken of every midshipman every year, usually available for purchase via mail by midshipmen and their families; plebes are photographed in formal dress blues (FDBs); upperclass are photographed in the uniform of their choice, though for firsties the yearbook picture must be in FDBs; lettermen also may be photographed in their letter sweaters.

class rank   See *order of merit.*

class ring   The ring; the process of designing, selecting, and ordering begins at the end of youngster year; since 1869 every class, except those of 1877–80, has had its own design; officially sanctioned on a midshipman's finger at the Ring Dance; worn with the class crest facing inward and the Academy seal facing outward until graduation, when the position is reversed.

class size   (1) Average number of students in an academic or professional class is 17.5; the number usually falls somewhere between 10 and

22. (2) Average number of students in a graduating class is normally around 975.

CMOD Pronounced "see-mod." Acronym for company mate of the deck, a plebe or youngster standing watch in a company area; also called the mate.

CNN badge See *National Service Defense Medal.*

CO Pronounced "see-oh." (1) Navy-wide term, short for commanding officer. (2) Short for Company Officer.

Coast Guard Academy The U.S. Coast Guard Academy in New London, Connecticut.

coastie Nickname for a member of the U.S. Coast Guard Academy.

Colorado Country Club Nickname for the U.S. Air Force Academy.

color company Company with the most accumulated color points for everything from academics and athletics to parades and military activities; color points are awarded to stimulate rivalry among the companies; the winning company is honored during Commissioning Week; throughout the following academic year, midshipmen in the winning company enjoy certain privileges, including the right to wear a gold E (for excellence) on the flap of their uniform's left-hand breast pocket (see *chest candy, flare,* and *Joe pins*); most midshipmen consider the process of selecting a color company to be about 50 percent legitimate, 50 percent luck.

color girl See *color person.*

Color Parade Parade during Commissioning Week, at which the new color company is announced; the last parade for the first class; frequently the parade with the largest percentage of heat casualties. See also *Dedication Parade.*

color person (1) Formerly color girl; usually the girlfriend or fiancée of the fall company commander of the color company; to date, history records no color boy. (2) Individual whose uniform is the sharpest during a uniform inspection ("I was the color person today"); also called "color man."

colors Military-wide reference to the American flag and the raising and lowering of the flag; during colors, midshipmen on the Yard face in the direction of the flag, stand at attention, and—if in uniform—salute for the duration of the ceremony; the same thing happens on every American military installation worldwide.

come-around Instructional or training (or grilling) session for discipline or professional knowledge; a come-around involves a plebe and an

Plebes stand with their backs to a bulkhead during a come-around.
Courtesy of USNA

upperclass, following which the upperclass may sign a paper attesting to the plebe's adequate performance and/or professional knowledge; another excuse for Joes to flame on plebes.

Commandant   U.S. Naval Academy's second-ranking military officer (after the Superintendent); essentially, the Commandant is the dean of military affairs—overseeing discipline and professional training; frequently called "the Dant."

Commandant's List   Made by about 22 percent of midshipmen; requirements are semester QPR of at least 2.9, at least a B in military performance, an A in conduct, at least a B in physical education; those qualifying wear no special insignia, but may, as upperclass, be awarded extra liberty.

Commissioning Week   Week in late May culminating with graduation; in short, one hell of a party. See Chapter 7 for more information.

company   Basic unit of organization within the Brigade; each company has about 140 midshipmen.

company commander   A first class who is head of his or her company.

Company Officer   A commissioned officer in charge of a company.

company wardroom   Academy's equivalent of a civilian college's dormitory common room; located in a company area, it usually has a TV, VCR, DVD player, refrigerator, microwave, and other electric amenities; privileges to use it are conferred on the basis of one's Academy class or academic status and are defined by company policy as established by the company commander; plebes almost always have no (zero) wardroom privileges.

comp time   Short for compensatory time; usually a canceled class, sometimes during X-weeks, because the class meeting was accomplished during some other time (for example, film at night or exam).

computer   The Naval Academy issues each plebe a computer at the end of Plebe Summer; during their years at the Academy, midshipmen purchase their computers through payroll deduction and keep them upon graduation; the competition for this contract is stiff among computer companies.

conduct   (1) Commendable behavior. (2) The Academy's system of administrative discipline; officially, the administrative conduct system; see "Conduct" section in the Military chapter (Chapter 3).

Conduct Board   Board comprised of various superiors to which midshipmen must go if they have been repeat conduct offenders; not fun; possible outcomes can include separation.

con locker   Short for confidential locker; the only lockable locker in every midshipman's room.

A midshipmen puts on his full dress blues. Behind him his con-locker is visible.
Courtesy of USNA

core curriculum Required courses in engineering, the sciences, math, and the humanities; heavily weighted toward engineering, math, and science, the core curriculum constitutes the bulk of every midshipman's academic load.

corfams Pronounced "cor-a-frams." Black synthetic-leather shoes worn by many military personnel; needs no waxing; permits no foot to breathe.

counseling Formal discussion ("He counseled me on how to make my rack").

countdown Period beginning thirty-six or thirty (depending on the number of companies in the Brigade) days before Herndon when, on the day corresponding to its number (for example, the Fifteenth Company on the fifteenth day prior to Herndon), the plebes in that particular company perform some outrageously ridiculous act.

course load Every midshipman must take at least fifteen credit hours per semester; some take as many as twenty-one or twenty-two. During their four years at the Academy, midshipmen take a minimum of 140 credit hours—considerably more (perhaps 25 to 35 percent more) than students at most civilian colleges; midshipmen also add military performance, drill, physical education, and other military-related activities.

course policy statement Handed out on the first day of each course; written by the instructor, it gives information and guidelines regarding the course as well as an instructor's policy statement outlining the teacher's practices and expectations in his or her particular class.

cover When used as a noun, means a midshipman's hat, worn year-round since 1956; tradition has it that a member of the opposite sex who dons a midshipman cover owes the owner of the hat a kiss—mothers of midshipmen love to do this, much to many midshipmen's chagrin. When used as a verb, means that midshipman requests or does indicate another's presence (accountability) at taps, lectures, or room visits ("Cover for me"); illegal and an honor offense.

CQPR Pronounced "see-kyooper." Acronym for cumulative quality point rating. See *GPA* and *order of merit.*

Crabtown Nickname for Annapolis.

crash and burn A term decreasing in use; to perform poorly; to get the short end of the stick; to get hosed, to bite it, to die; to get shot down, as on a date.

crewba (1) Affectionate term used by members of the women's crew team toward one another. (2) Incredibly derogatory term used by

A midshipman lines up his shot during the annual croquet match against St. John's College.
Courtesy of USNA

non-members of the woman's crew team toward female rowers; see *WUBA*.

croquet Since 1982 an annual match with St. John's College; it is unclear which is more important: the match or the associated parties.

crypto Short for (1) the cryptology community and (2) a member of said community.

dad See *mom (or dad)*.

D&B Short for the drum and bugle corps, formally established in 1925; sometimes referred to by the rest of the Brigade as "beaters and blowers."

the Dant See *Commandant*.

Dant's List See *Commandant's List*.

Dark Ages Period between Christmas and spring break characterized by cold temperatures, snow, rain, and overwhelmingly poor attitudes; easily the most depressing period of the academic year.

dark side From the movie *Star Wars;* a phrase connoting the dating of another midshipman ("He [or she] has gone over to the dark side"). See *slayer.*

Midshipmen walk to class during the Dark Ages, the period between January and spring break.
Courtesy of USNA

dating   Rules govern dating. (1) Plebes may date each other, unless both plebes are in the same company. (2) Plebes may date civilians—even the civilians they dated prior to I-Day, although it takes a special kind of relationship to survive four years by the bay (see *2% Club*). (3) Upperclass may not date plebes; and plebes may not date upperclass. (4) Upperclass may date other upperclass, unless both upperclass are in the same company; see *love chit*. (5) Public displays of affection (PDA) by midshipmen in uniform, on or off the Yard, are not acceptable—just as they are not acceptable in the fleet; midshipmen may escort members of the opposite sex by having the male offer his arm to the female, regardless of who is in uniform.

the days   Plebe rate consisting of the number of days to graduation, to the Ring Dance, to every major holiday including the next leave period, to the Army-Navy football game, to the next Army-Navy athletic contest, as well as any "special" days a particular upperclass (Joe) wants to hear (days to a mid's birthday, for example); "the days" often are given in response to an upperclass demand, for example, "Gimme the Days!" or "What are the Days."

dead week   Slang for the week prior to Commissioning Week.

dean   Usually referring to the Academy's Academic Dean and Provost, overseer of academics; sometimes another dean, either one of the foregoing's associates or the dean of admissions.

Dean's List   Made by about 15 percent of midshipmen; those not on Superintendent's List with a semester QPR of at least 3.4, with no failures in any course or professional area; those qualifying may wear a bronze star on certain uniforms.

deck   Navy-wide term for any floor or the ground.

Dedication Parade   One of two big parades during Commissioning Week; it honors the faculty. See also *Color Parade.*

Defense Language Institute (DLI)   Located at Monterey, California; school where select officers and enlisted personnel go for intense foreign language study.

demerits   Given on a sliding scale for a "fry," which consists—singly or in combination—of demerits, tours, extra duty, and restriction; the elemental units of punishment measuring a midshipman's failure to use good judgment or to meet standards; demerits are used (1) for determining semester conduct grades and (2) as threats for impending conduct action if performance does not improve.

dental   Short for the dental office located in Bancroft Hall's sixth wing; its services are available and free to all midshipmen; every midshipman receives an annual dental screening.

Dep Dant   Short for Deputy Commandant, the assistant to the Commandant.

detail   See *plebe detail.*

detailer   (1) Key player in determining every Navy and Marine Corps officer's career path by assisting in, and eventually assigning, officers' future duty assignments; called "monitors" in the Marine Corps. (2) Second class or firstie assigned to plebe detail.

device   Navy-wide term for insignia usually worn on the collars of uniforms.

dickover   Not-so-affectionate term for Rickover Hall and/or the classes that take place there.

dining in   Sit-down dinner such as one for a company, team, or extracurricular group, and restricted to the group's members. See also *dining out.*

dining out   Function, usually a dinner, for all the members of a company, team, or extracurricular group and their guests. See also *dining in.*

dirtbag   Slime ball; a filthy or uncouth person; a poor performer; the opposite of a Joe, and therefore (statistically) perhaps the majority of the Brigade. See also *shitbag.*

dive school   (1) Practice of throwing live mice caught in Bancroft Hall into toilets to see if they can swim; they can't. (2) U.S. Navy's school to teach SCUBA in Panama City, Florida (see *jump school*).

Dixie cup   Midshipman's sailor hat; edged in blue and worn only by plebes during Plebe Summer; the item plebes must pull off of Herndon and subsequently replace with a midshipman cover.

doolie   See *plebe.*

DOR   Navy-wide acronym for drop on request, wherein a participant in one mode of training requests—for whatever reason—transfer to another mode or quit; whether justified or not, the assumption often is negative, that is, the participant made the request because of lack of aptitude or desire or because he or she found the training too tough.

dork   Nerd; means the same thing at the Academy as it does anywhere else.

dork fork   Slang term for the small trident worn by Trident scholars on their working uniform shirts. See also *chest candy* and *flare.*

double agent   Academy graduate who, when classes are bigger, ranks below 999 in his or her class; not an academically smart person.

double E   (1) Nickname for electrical engineering, notoriously one of the Academy's most troublesome courses, especially for bull majors; see *cables* and *wires.* (2) Reference to the infamous cheating scandal in the fall of 1992 by the class of 1994 in wires, the results of which still linger; the scandal has dramatically affected how things are done at the Academy regarding honor and character development.

downtown   The town of Annapolis. See also *DTA.*

drag   (1) Candidate for the Naval Academy who is currently visiting the Yard. (2) Anyone taken to King Hall or around the Academy by a midshipman; usually derogatory. (3) See *get a ride.*

dream sheet   Navy-wide term for any form filled out by midshipmen or officers regarding their desired career path.

drill   Parade practice and/or march-on practice; usually several times a week on Dewey, Farragut, Rip Miller, or Worden fields for all midshipmen except in-season athletes, with additional practices for limited periods during the fall and spring; generally hated by most midshipmen. See also *parades.*

drop   (1) To get down on the floor or ground, usually for push-ups, now illegal at the Academy. (2) To cease taking an academic course or to cease playing a sport ("I dropped English this semester"). (3) To rescind ("My fry was dropped"), see *DOR*.

drunk eagles   Situation occurring when the eagles on the side buttons on the side screws of a midshipman's cover are crooked.

Drydock   Restaurant in Dahlgren Hall; used by faculty, midshipmen, and their guests. For more information, visit www.usna.edu/NAF/DryDock.

DTA   Acronym for downtown Annapolis; where upperclass hang out whenever they can.

dual major   Selection of two areas of academic concentration; possible, it may be undertaken with approval of the Academic Dean; some midshipmen do it, but it's extremely tough.

duty   See *on duty.*

duty section   Group of midshipmen in a company on duty for a day, headed by the company duty officer (CDO); from a Navy-wide term indicating the portion of a ship's personnel or squadron at duty stations and ready to react to emergencies.

duty station   Navy-wide term indicating a place of assignment. See also *station.*

EAFD   Acronym for many terms, both military and otherwise; including early airborne fighter defense, eat a fat doughnut, eat a fat duck.

eat by the numbers   Motivational technique occurring occasionally in King Hall in connection with plebe training; the practice of moving one's utensils to and from the mouth at right angles in four increments: fork up from plate to level of mouth is one, into mouth is two, out of mouth and back to spot directly above plate is three, back down to plate is four; not an official practice; usually used as punishment; practice is discouraged. See also *square meal.*

ECA   Acronym for extra-curricular activity.

e-course   Short for endurance course; a two-mile hilly course at the naval station across the Severn River.

ED   Acronym for extra duty.

e-fry   All "frys" are now e-frys, with notification of a conduct offense arriving in the midshipman's electronic inbox; as a rule, however, midshipmen believe that an e-fry without prior notification is a coward's way of frying someone; some Company Officers even require that midshipmen confront the individual being fryed prior to actually writing the fry on the computer. See also *fry* and *form 2*.

EI   Acronym for extra instruction; it is voluntary or mandatory, depending on academic status; a midshipman performing poorly in a class may be required to attend EI.

Eighth Wing Players   Now a legend in Bancroft Hall with midshipmen hoping for its eventual return; formerly (ending sometime in the late 1990s) an informal acting group, consisting primarily of midshipmen living in Bancroft's eighth wing who gave lightly rehearsed humorous skits in the eighth wing parking lot on Thursday nights before home football games; skits poked fun at Academy life including rules and sometimes Academy officials, for which (along with the interference of evening study time) the productions were canceled.

e-mail   Short for electronic mail; the way midshipmen communicate. See also *MIDS*.

EMI   Pronounced "ee-em-eye." Navy-wide acronym for extra military instruction; corrective instruction in cases of conduct or performance infractions; whether intended or not and whether legal or not, EMI is generally used as a punishment.

end of semester leave   After spring semester exams and prior to Commissioning Week; usually called intercessional leave.

evolution   Any activity that a midshipman has to do ("The lecture tonight is a mandatory evolution"). See also *MWOT*.

exams   The Naval Academy is on a semester system; exams are held before Christmas vacation (or leave) and in early May; exams generally last three hours; in most cases, midshipmen may depart for Christmas vacation following their last exam; they may also depart for end-of-semester leave following their last exam in May, but usually must return to the Academy for training and meetings prior to the beginning of Commissioning Week.

exchange student   Any of about half-a-dozen midshipmen who trade places with about half-a-dozen Air Force, Coast Guard, and West Point cadets during the first semester of their second class year.

excusal list   List of midshipmen released from an Academy obligation on the Yard because of special status. See also *movement order*.

extra duty   Also called ED; duty that may be assigned by the administrative conduct system as punishment and carried out when the normal working day is over (usually on Saturday afternoons); ED may vary according to the discretion of the individual overseeing the punishment, but it ordinarily consists of non-fatiguing upkeep, maintenance, and administrative tasks in and around Bancroft Hall. See also *EMI* and *demerits*.

eyes in the boat   Borrowed from the sport of rowing; for plebes, the act of keeping one's eyes set fixedly forward.

eyes in the boat machine   Any creation made either by plebes or upperclass restricting peripheral vision, ensuring that one's vision remain directly ahead.

Fac Rep   See *O-Rep*.

faculty   Teachers; the Academy has about 550 full-time faculty members; of that number, (1) about 15 percent are women and (2) about 50 percent are civilian (Note: the Air Force Academy and West Point have far lower percentages of civilian teachers, for better or for worse); there are no graduate teaching assistants; 70 percent of the civilian faculty is tenured; the civilian faculty's average number of years of service on the faculty is 12.3 (most members of the military faculty rotate through; some are permanent military professors who never leave); all civilian faculty have PhDs (with very few exceptions, some newly hired faculty have completed a dissertation but not yet defended it); about 66 percent of the military faculty have advanced degrees; faculty-student ratio is about one to seven.

fair winds and following seas   Navy-wide phrase for "good luck" or "good sailing"; usually heard at retirement ceremonies and funerals.

fall ball   Out-of-season interscholastic scrimmages in lacrosse and baseball.

farewell ball   Occurs just prior to graduation during Commissioning Week; the dance dates from 1865.

fat tables   Slang for battalion double ration tables, served at breakfast and lunch, for varsity athletes bulking up; also called "extra ration" tables. See also *cat-V*.

FDBs   Acronym for the full dress blue uniform; what midshipmen wear during dress parades; it is as comfortable as rough wool next to the skin can be, and half as breathable. See also *uniforms*.

"fidelity is up, obedience is down"   (1) plebe rate. (2) Saying that confirms whether a watch belt is being worn right side up.

fieldball   Basically a rule-less Academy intramural sport combining aspects of rugby, soccer, and lacrosse; apparently played only at the

Academy and at the New York State Penitentiary; a game some believe is still played to justify the need for an orthopedics department at the Academy.

fighter jock   Slang for a fighter pilot.

"find out and report back"   Something Joes say to plebes when the plebe uses the basic response, "I'll find out." See also *responses.*

fire it up   Sarcastically motivational phrase used by midshipmen.

first class alley   In King Hall, any aisle between tables and the bulkheads where only firsties may walk when going to and from tables. See also *second class alley.*

First Class Parents Weekend   Held in September; the first semi-organized visit by parents since Parents Weekend at the end of Plebe Summer, and the last until Commissioning Week.

firstie   Member of the first class; the equivalent of a senior at a civilian college. See also *plebe, youngster,* and *second class.*

five and dive   Slang phrase for serving the five-year obligation after graduation and then leaving the naval service ("I'm gonna five and dive").

flamer   Usually associated with plebe indoctrination; an upperclass who is excessively harsh on plebes; taken from the verb "to flame," meaning to go off, to grill, to yell, or to scream ("He flamed on me at tables").

flare   From the movie *Office Space;* flare refers to the quantity of buttons, pins, and/or chest candy on a uniform; flare comes in all kinds, from dork forks to stars to craftmaster pins to PRT wreaths to color company Es; an assumption made by midshipmen (unclear whether it is true or not) is that the more flare a given midshipman has, the more of a dork he or she is. See also *Joe pins.*

the fleet   The Navy and Marine Corps at large; the naval service; the "real" Navy.

flyboy   Military-wide nickname for a pilot.

FMF   Acronym for fleet marine force; the "real" Marine Corps.

FONA   Acronym for Friends of the Naval Academy.

FONA pass   FONA passes were established after September 11th to allow frequent visitors access to the Yard.

formals   See *alpha inspection* and *inspections.*

formation   Any assembling in ranks and taking a muster, but usually in reference to formations prior to morning and noon meals, and following Sunday dinner.

form 2 Written document (on the computer) that puts someone on report; today, everything is electronic and filled out online; similar to a demerit slip in high school. See also *e-fry* and *fry*.

Forrestal lecture Generally a once-a-semester address to the Brigade and public by a well-known speaker from outside the Academy; sometimes called by midshipmen a "snorrestal lecture" (from the verb "to snore") or a "bore-us-all lecture." See also *MWOT*.

Forrest Sherman Field (1) Formal, official name for the field on Hospital Point, the area across Dorsey Creek and below the cemetery and hospital. (2) Home airfield of the Blue Angels in Pensacola, Florida.

forty-year swim Forty-minute swim test in the first semester of second class year; it is performed in khaki shirt and pants; many midshipmen cannot imagine a more painful experience in the water that does not involve sharks.

Foundation Short for the U.S. Naval Academy Foundation; its fundamental purpose is to arrange and sometimes help finance an additional year at college or prep school for Academy candidates in order to strengthen their academics prior to admission. See Chapter 7 for more information.

four years together by the bay Phrase referring sometimes affectionately but more often sarcastically to midshipmen's years at the Academy; taken from the third verse of "Navy Blue and Gold."

frat See *fraternization*.

fraternization (1) Navy-wide term meaning undue familiarity within the chain of command, possibly resulting in special favors. (2) At the Academy, dating within a company or the dating of an upperclass and a plebe (see *dating*); also, condition wherein any upperclass is too friendly with a plebe.

freight train/freight training Practice of attacking someone when he or she is sleeping; when someone is sleeping on his or her back, the instigator puts either one or two dim flashlights over the sleeper's eyes or near the face while making freight train whistle noises increasing in volume; when the sleeper opens his or her eyes, another person hits the sleeper (usually very hard) in the face with a pillow to simulate being hit by the oncoming freight train; similar to "mack truck," but with different associated sounds.

frog Slang for a pinch clip for the spindle backs of uniform nametags and medals.

fry   Indictment and/or accusation of an infraction in the administrative conduct system; its penalties are many, including demerits and/or restriction; frys come in two forms: minor and major offenses, with a corresponding list of acceptable punishments for each; see the Military chapter (Chapter 3) for a full discussion. When used as a verb, means to put (or be put) on report. See also *e-fry* and *form 2*.

fry trap   Nickname for a restriction muster or any situation with especially high potential for disciplinary trouble. See also *fry*.

FTN   Acronym for a number of common phrases, the most frequently used, however, is "f°°° the Navy"; usually said when extremely down on (1) the Navy, (2) the Academy, or (3) both.

FUBAR   Military-wide acronym for f°°°ed up beyond all repair; a completely unsalvageable mess, from which recovery is unlikely; a gordian knot. See also *CF* and *SNAFU*.

fuct   E-mail and instant messenger spelling of what midshipmen consider "a frequent midshipman situation."

galley   (1) Navy-wide term for any kitchen. (2) Restaurant in the visitor center, primarily for tourists; see *Drydock*.

garrison cap   Military-wide name for any pointed, brimless hat; at the Academy, the pointed khaki hat worn only during the summer and only by upperclass; often called a "piss-cutter." See also *uniforms*.

gates   The U.S. Naval Academy has three operating gates: Gate 1 (the main gate), Gate 3, and Gate 8; each has a guardhouse and guards who are enlisted Marines based at the naval station across the Severn River.

gate watcher   Midshipman who stands at a gate on any given night looking for infractions by returning midshipmen; usually someone on duty because only a Joe would watch a gate if he or she were not on duty.

Gate Zero   Pedestrian gate behind Halsey Field House; used for food deliveries and little else.

geek   One who studies all the time; one who has few social skills; a dork.

geekers   Eyeglass frames issued to all midshipmen requiring eyesight correction; often called, because of their effect on the opposite sex, birth control glasses.

get a brace   See *brace up*.

get a ride   When a plebe wins the privilege of not having to chop up and down stairways or through passageways in Bancroft Hall when accompanied by an upperclass; also, "give a ride," that is, for an upperclass to do so; more frequently called "dragging."

gig line Theoretical line made on a uniform by aligning the overlap of the shirt with the end of the belt and the overlap of the fly ("Jones, straighten your gig line").

goat court Either of two enclosed areas of Bancroft Hall formed by Bancroft's third wing in the First Regiment and by Bancroft's fourth wing in the Second Regiment; the windows facing the goat courts look onto a lower roof below; within the courts, noises echo seemingly forever.

go fasters (1) Running shoes issued Plebe Summer that no one ever seems to wear again. (2) Generic term for any running sneakers.

"Go Navy, sir!" One of two cries shouted by plebes when they square corners; the other is "Beat Army, sir!"

good to go Term used by midshipmen indicating they are ready to go; sometimes heard as GTG (pronounced "gee-ta-gee").

gouge When used as a noun, means assistance; the essential shortcut information on any subject; the answers ("Gimme the gouge"); sometimes called "goo-hay"; gouge information from past tests and papers is illegal. Also used as a verb ("Gouge me").

GPA Acronym for grade point average; it averages academic grades only, and is determined by (1) multiplying each course's grade (four points for an A, three points for a B, two points for a C, one point for a D, zero points for an F) by the number of credits for that course (the number of credits usually equals the number of hours the course meets each week), (2) adding those products, and (3) dividing that sum by the sum of the credits. See also *CQPR* and *QPR*.

grab-and-go Designated area of King Hall where upperclass usually returning from athletic competition or practice may get sandwiches, fruit, and other food items for carry-out at dinner time.

grade point average See *GPA* and *QPR*.

graduation Day in late May when hats are thrown into the air; what it's all about; happiness incarnate.

graduation requirements Requirements are a cumulative grade point average of 2.0, a C (beginning with the class of 1967); minimum of 140 credit hours; complete or validate all the stipulated courses in the selected major; satisfy all academic, military, and physical education requirements; contrary to widespread belief, neither Ds—even

New graduates toss their hats.
Courtesy of USNA

in one's major—nor final semester grades averaging below 2.0 automatically prevent a firstie from graduating.

graduation salute   First salute given by a new ensign or second lieutenant following graduation; by custom, the recipient of the salute receives a silver dollar.

grape   Marine Corps term for the cranium or head ("Use your grape!").

grappling   Slang for the wrestling aspect of physical education.

gravy   Small numerical fraction in a midshipman's CQPR that makes him or her sat; according to *Reef Points,* "The 0.001 of a 2.001 CQPR."

gray hull   Any Navy ship (surface or sub); all midshipmen will graduate with at least one gray hull cruise under their belt.

green beach   Outside edge of the roof of Bancroft Hall, where midshipmen sometimes go to catch some rays; illegal. See also *red beach.*

grill   When used as a verb, means what a flamer or a Joe does—in short, yelling at plebes. When used as a noun, a Marine Corps term for teeth ("He got punched in the grill").

groups I, II, III   The three possible groups in which a midshipman can select a major; group I is technical engineering majors; group II is general sciences; group III is humanities majors, which is also known and referred to as "bull majors."

hair   The Naval Academy follows standard Navy regulations regarding hair, except the Academy (like the Marine Corps) much more rigorously enforces such regulations. (1) For men: after Plebe Summer (they are all shorn on I-Day) hair must be tapered in the back and on the sides, and no longer than four inches on top. (2) For women: during plebe year hair must be no longer than the bottom of the collar; after that they have no hair length requirement, but when in uniform their hair must be worn "up" and must not impede the wearing of the cover; see *two-inch bulk rule.* (3) On paper, midshipmen are forbidden to give haircuts to other midshipmen, but many do anyway. (4) Hairpieces and limited afros are legal.

the Hall   See *Bancroft.*

hall brawl   A rumble, plebes against upperclass taking place in Bancroft Hall; illegal.

hall rat   Midshipman who stays in Bancroft Hall on weekends; one with limited, or no, social life. See also *geek* and *Joe Mid.*

halo effect   Benefits (or glow) deriving from a good first impression, thus charming the midshipman. See also *reverse halo effect.*

hand to gland   Decreasing in use, a slang term used to describe "hand to hand," the self-defense training aspect of physical education for second class. See also *grappling.*

happiness factor   A now rarely used term indicating the ratio of the number of days of a forthcoming leave to the number of days until that leave.

hard charger   Slang for a very motivated person; usually used sarcastically.

hate chit   Slang term similar to a love chit in that it removes someone from a company, but opposite in the reason why someone leaves; the process a midshipman goes through to change companies because (1) he or she either received bad or seemingly unfair treatment or (2) believes he or she is strongly disliked by company mates to a degree that it affects working relationships within the company; this is the last line of defense for a midshipmen who does not get along with others and as a result, very rarely happens.

haze gray and underway   Navy-wide phrase referring to (1) the actual or anticipated benefits of being an officer in the surface fleet; see *SWO;*

(2) actually under way ("The last line is untied; we're haze gray and under way").

hazing   Absolutely forbidden.

head   Navy-wide term for a toilet.

head gouge   (1) Any reading material taken with a midshipman who plans on spending an extended period of time in the head for any reason. (2) Actual publication comprised of relevant issues placed in bathrooms in Bancroft Hall for midshipmen to read, since everyone goes there.

head restrictee   Also called "senior restrictee"; midshipman in charge of accountability at restriction musters; he or she is the midshipman with the most number of days remaining on restriction until those days have been served; a rank perceived by some as an honor, especially if it is the highest rank one achieves as a midshipman. See also *slide.*

heads-up   Borrowed from baseball, a phrase meaning "look out!" or "look up!"; a bringing of something to someone's attention; a notification or warning ("I'll give you a heads-up when the stripers are in the company area").

height and weight restrictions   (1) Seventy-eight inches (6'6") is the maximum height for commissioning; that standard may be waived, but anyone exceeding it usually faces limited service options. (2) Any midshipman exceeding weight standards may be dismissed, but seldom is.

helicopter   God's gift to aviation.

Herndon   Symbolic end of plebe year, and an early event during Commissioning Week. See Chapter 7 for more information.

HERO   Acronym for human education resource officer; from *Reef Points:* "provides support to the chain of command relating to human relations issues, and to help resolve peer issues within the company."

high and tight   Typical Marine Corps haircut, consisting of closely cropped hair on the top of the head and essentially shaved hair (bald) on the sides; cause for ridicule for many people. See also *landing strip.*

hit the wall   To reach one's point of exhaustion, as in an athletic event or in preparing for an exam ("in the PRT, I hit the wall and couldn't do any more push-ups" or "In preparing for my double E final, I hit the wall at 4 AM and fell into the rack"); to be unable to do more. See also *bonk.*

HO Pronounced "ayche-oh." Acronym for honor offense, essentially a violation of the honor concept.

Ho Chi Minh From the Ho Chi Minh Trail in Vietnam; the tunnel labyrinth for the Academy's steam heating system, frequently used by plebes to accomplish recons throughout the Yard.

holidays As federal employees, midshipmen receive all federal holidays (Labor Day, Columbus Day, Veterans Day, Martin Luther King Day, Presidents Day); they also receive two weekdays at Thanksgiving, two to three weeks at Christmas, and nine days (including weekends) for spring break.

honor committee Stripers from each battalion selected by the Superintendent and Commandant to investigate alleged honor offenses; when members of the committee are designated as an honor board, they make recommendations to the Commandant regarding disposition. See also *honor nazi.*

honor concept Much more complex than it once was, it still essentially suggests that midshipmen should not lie, cheat, or steal; written by midshipmen for midshipmen—the only service academy to have an honor concept that is completely run by the students. For more information see "Honor" section in the Military chapter (Chapter 3).

honor nazi Slang for any midshipman who is especially diligent in searching for honor offenses; considered by some to be "flaming Joes." See also *reg hound.*

hook When used as a noun, means the preferred one, the one to get ("That class is the hook!"). When used as a verb, means to give or receive assistance or the blessed benefit of the doubt ("Hook me on the math assignment" or "The prof hooked him with an A").

hook up To get together in any capacity, from kissing to more involved activity, with a member of the opposite sex ("Mary and John hooked up last night after the dance").

"HOO-YAH!" SEAL motivational call; not to be confused with "OO-RAH!"

hot seat At tables, the seat next to the squad leader; always occupied by a plebe. See also *smack.*

Hospital Point Quasi-peninsula where the medical clinic is located, as well as Forrest Sherman Field.

hound Monger; one constantly looking for something to an excessive degree, usually to a fault, such as a gouge hound or a reg hound; usually carries negative connotations.

Hudson High   Nickname for West Point.

Hudson hips   Sometimes imaginary weight gain phenomenon similar to the "freshman fifteen" affecting cadets (of both sexes) at West Point. See also *Severn River hip disease.*

100s night   Occurs on a February night, one hundred days from graduation; for several hours plebes switch places with firsties; seldom observed.

I-ball   See *international ball.*

I believe button   Imaginary button many midshipmen push upon recognizing something will not be logically understood—ever ("After seeing that physics proof on the board and still not understanding it, I pushed the I believe button").

ice cream suit   Slang for a midshipman's short-sleeved summer white uniform with shoulder boards, the warm-weather counterpart of SDBs. See also *uniforms.*

ICOR   Acronym for in charge of room; primarily a designation for plebes, the midshipman who has that responsibility for the day or moment, and who takes the brunt for any infraction.

I-Day   Induction day; the day the Academy experience begins; sometimes referred to as "the hottest day of the year."

IHTFP   Acronym for several declarations common to midshipmen, the most prevalent and one used probably at least once by every midshipman prior to graduation is, "I hate this f***ing place"; other less common and invariably sarcastic phrases associated with this acronym are, "I'm here to fly planes," "I'm here to fail physics," "I hope there's a Friday parade," and "I have truly found paradise." See also *BOHICA.*

Ike jacket   Short, lightweight jacket worn throughout the Navy and at the Academy with various uniforms; the name derives from the former president who was a lover of this particular style of jacket and apparently wore one all the time.

ILS   Acronym for inflated lat syndrome; a condition sometimes plaguing midshipmen, usually accentuated by the wearing of overly tight shirts and a propensity to look at oneself in weight room mirrors.

indoc   System of professional development and indoctrination of plebes; often called "plebe indoc"; considered by some (mostly plebes) to be hell on earth.

inner (and outer)   (1) A run around the Yard's inner perimeter, about 3 miles. (2) A run around the inside of the Yard's outer perimeter,

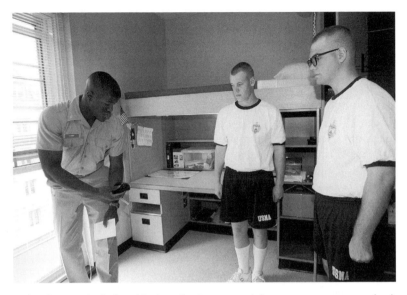

A detailer uses balled-up black socks during an alpha room inspection to check for dust.
Courtesy of USNA

about 4.5 miles. Visit www.usna.edu/PEScheds/running_routes.pdf for a map of these routes.

inspections   Among the many are the personnel inspection (of a midshipman and his or her uniform at company, watch, or restriction formation), haircut inspection, walk-through inspection (of midshipmen's rooms during the day or of midshipmen at formation), alpha inspection (white-glove, black-sock formal room inspection—also called "formals" and "room formals"), and seabag inspection; the rooms of plebes (and indeed all midshipmen) generally are inspected daily and are expected to be kept at "bravo" standards.

intel   Short for the intelligence community. See also *spook*.

intercessional   One of three periods (prior to reform, following Christmas vacation, and prior to Commissioning Week) in which midshipmen have lots to do, usually meetings, briefs, and lectures. See also *MWOT*.

intercessional leave   See *end of semester leave*.

international ball   Spring Brigade-wide dance that draws foreign officers and embassy personnel from the international community, as well as foreign exchange students from nearby schools. See also *hook up*.

IP   See *Irish pennant.*

Irish pennant   From *Reef Points:* "An unseamanlike, dangling loose end of a line or piece of clothing"; hence, on a uniform, it would be lint or a loose thread that suggests lack of neatness; while still used Navy-wide, it is no longer sanctioned because of its potential to offend those of Irish descent.

jacket   (1) Article of clothing. (2) Military-wide term for any file in any division or department containing records or information about an individual; at the Academy, the registrar permanently maintains all midshipman transcripts of grades, for example; all Academy-specific jackets are destroyed two years following graduation.

jarhead   Derogatory nickname for a Marine. See also *high and tight.*

jet jockey   Military-wide nickname for a fighter pilot.

jewelry   Watches are okay; discreet necklaces and religious medallions are okay if they cannot be seen when in uniform; rings are okay (limited to one per hand); anklets are not okay; bracelets and earrings are not okay for men unless they are medical or POW/MIA (Prisoner of War/Missing in Action) bracelets; discreet gold ball earrings (limited to one per lobe) are okay for women.

JID   Acronym for Joe in disguise; this is a person who appears to be on your side, who may even appear to support a possible infraction of given rules, who will then probably turn you in anyway. See also *Joe Mid.*

jimmy legs   Slang and derogatory term for the Naval Academy's Department of Defense police who provide security within the Yard; the term derived from the police driving GMC Jimmys, an early sport utility vehicle (SUV); instead of chasing delinquent midshipmen on foot, they would chase them on their "jimmy legs" and still sometimes not catch the midshipmen.

JO   Pronounced "jay-oh." Navy-wide term for junior officer, any officer new or comparatively new to the officer corps.

Joe   See *Joe Mid.*

Joe Gish   No longer around. See *W. T. Door.*

Joe Mid   When used as a noun, refers to the guy or girl who has taken Joe Gish and W. T. Door's place; a stickler for all the rules; not well liked; see *tool;* a saying regarding Joes is: "High school zeroes to Naval Academy heroes"; Joes are certainly a minority and usually are very aware of their Joeness and continue to act like Joes anyway; the term

"Joe" has nothing to do with academics; it is strictly a reference to the overzealous adherence to any and all regulations, which is why those who bend or break rules (probably the majority of midshipmen) tend to really dislike Joes. When used as an adjective, "Joe" is a modifier for anything Joes use to do Joe stuff, for example, a "Joe clipboard," a "Joe PDA," or a "Joe book."

Joe pins Another name for chest candy and flare; the supposition being that the more of these worn, the more of a "Joe" a given midshipman is likely to be.

Johnny A term decreasing in use; refers to a student at St. John's College.

joke jail Every Friday plebes are responsible for telling a joke at lunch; if jokes are deemed poor, they can be placed in joke jail by upperclass, where they must sit facing forward with their fork in front of and very close to their face to simulate the cell bars; they may not leave the table until they have been released from jail. See also *solitary confinement.*

jump school (1) Practice of throwing live mice caught in Bancroft Hall out of windows to see if they can fly; they can't. (2) The military's parachute school, run by the U.S. Army, that is located in Fort Benning, Georgia. See also *dive school.*

King Hall In Navy terms, the mess—the equivalent of an enormous officer's wardroom on a ship; where the midshipmen eat, in squads (unless at team tables), twelve to a table; shaped in the form of a T; plebes always face away from the anchor—or away from the middle of the T; King Hall can feed the entire Brigade in several minutes; rightly or wrongly, known by the midshipmen for sub-par food.

knockabout Any small sailing craft of the type used by the Academy for instruction and recreation; known for traveling considerably slower than the speed of sound.

Labyrinth The U.S. Naval Academy's literary magazine.

ladder Navy-wide term for any stairway or set of stairs.

landing strip Thin area of scalp on the top of the head seen when one gets a "high and tight."

late lights Practice of plebes staying up past taps with signed permission from their squad leader. See also *lights out* and *taps.*

leatherneck (1) Military-wide nickname for a Marine. (2) Rigorous summer training option for rising firsties interested in the U.S. Marine Corps.

leave   heaven; authorization for extended absence from the Academy, notably for Thanksgiving, Christmas, spring break, and summer vacations; leave generally begins after the last scheduled exam or last military obligation (LMO); midshipmen can also take emergency leave for the death or severe illness of a family member. See also *liberty*.

left hand salute   Variation of the tradition whereby midshipmen salute other midshipmen who have an attractive date; the left hand salute is rendered to a midshipman with a less-than-attractive date; the date thinks you are being respectful while the midshipmen knows you're making fun of him (and his date). See also *saluting*.

LES   Navy-wide acronym for a leave and earnings statement; now mostly computerized and online, this is the critical monthly document telling Navy personnel how much money they have (or don't have).

liberty   Authorization for midshipmen to depart Bancroft Hall or the Yard for a comparatively short time (not more than ninety-six hours); the specifics of particular kinds of liberty change like the wind depending on particular administrations. See also *leave*.

liberty hound   Midshipman who always craves liberty, perhaps to a fault if his or her liberty denies others' liberty.

lib-o   Short for liberty.

libs   Short for liberty ("I've got libs this weekend").

lights out   For plebes, at 11 PM; there are no lights out for upperclass. Also see *late lights* and *taps*.

line officer   Navy or Marine Corps officer eligible to succeed to command at sea; line officers wear stars on their sleeves; firsties also wear a star on their sleeves even though they are neither commissioned nor line officers.

LMO   Acronym for last military obligation.

lock and load   Taken from the process of getting a weapon ready to fire; term means to get ready ("Hey. Lock and load. He's coming for inspection").

locked on   Adjectival phrase describing a midshipman who is extremely motivated and pro-Academy ("I didn't know you were so locked on that you would attend a softball game on a Saturday").

lock it up   Usually said with one fist held clenched above one's head; means, quite simply, "Shut up!"

log   Military-wide term referring to a book or ledger for the recording of data or events during a watch.

The Log A now underground monthly midshipman humor magazine that usually pokes fun at the Academy. See also *Salty Sam* and *Eighth Wing Players*.

lose your ass To lose a bet, usually in reference to a plebe; until released by the winning upperclass, the losing plebe must request permission to do practically anything regarding his posterior; one would lose his or her ass only if he or she answered the question, "Do you bet your ass?" in the affirmative, and lost.

love chit Chit submitted for moving a midshipman out of a company to another because of a dating relationship within the original company; because some people believe that they can't control who they fall in love with, midshipmen sometimes date members of their same company, which is against the rules; when this happens, one of the offending parties must move companies; a love chit is submitted that states their affection and their desire to have one of them move companies; upon approval, the Company Officer finds one member of the couple a new home so the relationship can continue. See also *hate chit*.

Lucky Bag From the term for a ship's locker used for stowing miscellaneous confiscated, lost, or adrift items; the Academy yearbook, first published in 1894; reputedly the nation's largest, it contains highlights of the year plus pictures and home addresses of all graduating firsties; all midshipmen are offered an opportunity to authorize the requisitioning of their pay to buy a copy; parents and/or guardians of firsties receive forms to purchase their own; if purchased, it arrives by mail late in the fall following graduation.

mac-d Short for Macdonough Hall.

mack truck/mac trucking Practice of attacking someone when he or she is sleeping; when someone is sleeping on his or her back, the instigator puts either one or two dim flashlights over the sleeper's eyes or near the face while making big rig horn noises increasing in volume; when the sleeper opens his or her eyes, another person hits the sleeper (usually very hard) in the face with a pillow to simulate being hit by the oncoming mack truck. See also *freight train*.

main-o Short for main office, overseen by the OOW and assisted by the MOOW, a three-striper or above.

major (1) Midshipman's area of academic concentration, selected in the spring of plebe year; see *groups I, II, III*. (2) Significant conduct violation, worse than a minor.

mameluke   U.S. Marine Corps sword; a good graduation gift for newly commissioned Marine Corps officers.

mandatory   Must do. See also *mando.*

mando   Pronounced "man-dough." Short for mandatory, usually used as an adjective ("I've got a mando meal tonight"). See also *MWOT.*

MAPR   Pronounced "may-per." Acronym for midshipman academic performance report; usually written by professors on a mid who is struggling in a class (D or F); when written for outstanding performance, called a "positive MAPR."

march-over   Process of the Brigade marching from the Yard to Navy–Marine Corps Memorial Stadium prior to home football games; not usually enjoyed by midshipmen, other than admiring the sometimes attractive public.

Marine   One of the few, the proud; midshipmen may choose to become either Navy or Marine Corps officers upon graduation.

marlinspike seamanship   (1) Art and science of tying nautical knots for practical or decorative purposes. (2) Non-engine sailboating, the variety the Academy teaches.

Masqueraders   Academy's drama club; the oldest Academy extracurricular organization, tracing its roots to 1849; believed to be the nation's oldest collegiate theater group.

mate   See *CMOD.*

matrix   (1) Computer grid or spreadsheet, generally based on a midshipman's major, showing his or her required courses, possible electives, course offerings, and vacant periods for the remaining semesters; a particularly important instrument during pre-registration and registration by midshipmen and their academic advisers; the phrase (a) "she's ahead of her matrix" means that because of validation or transfer credits, she has room to take either an elective or a lighter course load; (b) "behind the matrix" generally means that because of a failed course or other academic trouble, a mid will likely be attending summer school. (2) Series of popular films (starring Keanu Reeves) that many midshipmen love.

max'd   Obtaining a perfect score on anything, but most frequently referring to the PRT ("He max'd it!").

McDonald's ribbon   See *National Service Defense Medal.*

MCMO   Acronym for midshipman in charge of main office; a firstie directing plebes and youngsters, generally main office messengers (MOMs).

mech-e   Slang for mechanical engineering; widely regarded as one of the most difficult majors.

Medal of Honor room   Any of numerous rooms in Bancroft Hall named for Academy graduates who won the Medal of Honor, each having a plaque and photograph outside the particular room.

medical   Place to go if you're sick or physically broken; there exist many different clinics, and even twenty-four-hour emergency care; all midshipmen receive free medical and dental care; they are given annual medical examinations; serious prolonged illnesses and injuries often are treated at Bethesda Naval Hospital near Washington, D.C.; serious emergencies may be treated at other local civilian health care facilities.

Mem Hall   Short for Memorial Hall; part of Bancroft Hall; dedicated to naval and Marine Corps heroes and Academy alumni killed in combat, all of whose names are displayed; it is a museum, and many people treat it like a library (they whisper); covers and hats are removed except by those on duty; now the site of various Academy functions, symposiums, and retirements.

Merchant Marine Academy   The U.S. Merchant Marine Academy, located in King's Point (Long Island), New York.

MFSD   Midshipmen food services department; also used to refer to the people who run and work in King Hall.

mice   Real ones; they are Bancroft Hall's most tenured, most adaptable, most tenacious, most resilient residents; catching them ranks among the midshipmen's relentless pursuits. See also *dive school* and *jump school*.

micromanager   Generally disliked individual who has to oversee every detail of a project; some midshipmen (rightly or wrongly) believe this to be generally synonymous with Company Officer (and sometimes other Academy officials as well).

mid (mids)   Short for midshipman (midshipmen); acceptable terms; do not use "middy" or "middies."

middy (middies)   Unacceptable nicknames for midshipmen, particularly the latter form; mids hate them and will probably tell you they do; use "mid" or "mids" (plural) instead.

mid hound   Non-midshipman female (or male) looking for a male (or female) midshipman to date; also known as "squid bait."

mid hunter   Synonym for mid hound.

midiot   Any midshipman not exercising the full capacity of his or her brain; common.

midn   Common and acceptable abbreviation for midshipman in written forms of communication.

mid rats   Short for mid rations; a fleet term used to describe food served late at night (near midnight) for those getting off watch; at the Naval Academy it primarily refers to box lunches, which most midshipmen don't like, usually calling them "box nasty."

mid regs   Short for midshipmen regulations; conduct expectations as specified in *Midshipmen Regulations,* which contains the disciplinary rules governing all aspects of midshipman life; *Midshipmen Regulations* is now available online at www.usna.edu/Commandant/Directives/Instructions/Instructions/COMDTMIDNINST%205400.6C.pdf.

MIDS   Acronym for Midshipman Information Data System; Web site and online database used for practically everything midshipmen do at the Academy; not open to the public.

midshipchick   Occasional slang term for a female midshipman; decreasing in use.

midshipman   Term applied to each student at the U.S. Naval Academy; it dates from the British Navy in the late seventeenth century, when young men training to be officers frequently were assigned to stations on the deck about midway between the bow and stern; also, the rank USNA students hold in the Navy; a midshipman is neither an officer nor enlisted, but between the two; most become line officers upon commissioning at graduation.

midslang   Variation of Midspeak.

Midspeak   U.S. Naval Academy vernacular; language peculiar to midshipmen and those who know about and work at the Academy.

midstang   Car of choice most midshipmen purchase after receiving their second class loan; not necessarily a Mustang, these range from the utilitarian to the jalopy to the insanely expensive, shiny variety.

Midstore   Short for Midshipmen Store; the Academy's campus store; it is the primary place where midshipmen do their shopping; a sprawling store that offers everything most major department stores offer, and then some.

mile-and-a-half   Part of the PRT, a run for time required of all midshipmen every semester; it usually is conducted outside around Farragut or Dewey fields.

miniature   Small copy of the class ring, sometimes given as an engagement ring; rarely, but sometimes purchased by female midshipmen as their class ring.

mini-BUD/S   Summer-option four-week taste of BUD/S for those rising firsties thinking of the SEALs as a warfare specialty selection.

minor   (1) Academic subspecialty, usually in a foreign language discipline. (2) Minor conduct infraction, less than a major.

MIR   Acronym for midshipman in ranks; any firstie who does not hold an official job.

misery hall   Trainer/first aid areas of Macdonough Hall and Halsey Field House; where damaged athletes go for repair.

MISLO   Acronym for midshipmen information systems liaison officer; in short, the person in each company who fixes other people's computers.

mo board   Short for maneuvering board; polar coordinate graph paper used in some navigation and leadership courses and on YPs; used extensively in the fleet to compute ship movements.

MOM   Pronounced "mom." Acronym for main office messenger, usually a plebe.

mom (or dad)   Decreasing in use, a reference to a midshipman's Company Officer.

Monterey   Short for the Navy's postgraduate school in Monterey, California, where many midshipmen eventually go as officers for advanced study but not immediately following graduation from the Academy.

An officer demonstrates a maneuvering board (mo board) problem for her class.
Courtesy of USNA

morning quarters   Before-breakfast accountability (attendance) formations in company areas.

Mother B   Dated nickname for Bancroft Hall; this is the place where Joe Gish and W. T. Door lived; because they're no longer around, the term isn't either.

motivator   Someone who loves to do what he or she is supposed to do; someone who does the right thing, always; usually used sarcastically.

movement order   Listing of those midshipmen authorized to participate in a special event outside the Yard.

Mrs. Supe   Supe's (superintendent's) wife.

multiple guess   Slang for a multiple-choice test.

murder boards   When firsties in a particular company convene to determine the performance grades of the three other classes; only so many can get As, so many Bs, and so many Cs.

music   What plebes fondly remember listening to in high school; additionally, what many of them listen to lovingly at sponsor houses.

muster   (1) Any roll call, or a formal taking of attendance (accountability) for meetings, taps, formations, etc.—usually in ranks. (2) Restriction muster: a requirement, as punishment, for midshipmen on restriction to assemble at a designated time and place in an inspection-ready uniform.

mutiny   Condition declared when an upperclass discovers more than four plebes in a room; the plebes are forced to go into the shower with their clothes on; exception: a mutiny cannot be declared if the room contains an American flag; illegal, but practiced anyway.

MWOT   Pronounced "em-watt." Acronym for mandatory waste of time.

MWR   Navy-wide acronym for Morale, Welfare, and Recreation; an organization raising money and coordinating events intended to boost the morale, welfare, and recreation of Navy personnel.

NAAA   Pronounced "n-triple a." Acronym for the Naval Academy Athletic Association, which organizes, promotes, and assists in financing Academy athletic programs.

NAFAC   Acronym for the annual week-long Naval Academy Foreign Affairs Conference; held in the spring, it attracts prominent speakers and college students from across the country. For more information, visit www.usna.edu/NAFAC.

NAMI   Pronounced "nammy." Acronym for the Naval Aeronautical Medical Institute; by extension, the series of medical tests, pokes, and prods prospective aviators take in Pensacola; because of the high failure rate, known widely as the "NAMI whammy."

NAPS Acronym for the Naval Academy Prep School in Newport, Rhode Island; about two hundred midshipmen enter the Academy from the one-year NAPS program each year.

NAPster Anyone attending, or a midshipman who attended, NAPS.

Narc (1) Short for naval architecture, or for a midshipman majoring in it. (2) Term borrowed from the Drug Enforcement Agency, to turn someone in to the authorities ("He narced me").

NASP Acronym for Naval Academy Summer Program; also, shortened term for the entity that oversees all midshipmen at the Academy during the summer (except plebes and those on plebe detail); those under NASP are primarily midshipmen attending summer school or those on restriction; because temptations are so great in Annapolis during the summer, widely regarded as possibly the Academy's biggest fry trap.

NASS Acronym for the Naval Academy Sailing Squadron, headquartered at the Robert Crown Sailing Center.

National Service Defense Medal Ribbon sanctioned for all military personnel—including midshipmen—for being active duty members of the armed forces during (1) the 1991 Gulf War and (2) the war on terror; also called CNN badge because midshipmen watched unfolding events primarily on CNN; also called the McDonald's ribbon because of its red and yellow colors, similar to the fast food restaurant colors; was referred to as the "Alive in '65" badge when it was given during the Vietnam War.

nav Short for any navigation course; the Academy requires a course in coastal piloting, ship handling, and celestial navigation for graduation.

the nav Short for the Navy.

the naval service The fleet; the Navy at large.

naval station Located across the Severn River; exists primarily to support the Naval Academy.

N.A.V.Y. Acronym for never again volunteer yourself; term usually associated with times when "the nav" is making a midshipman feel downhearted.

negative Military-wide term for "no." See also *affirmative*.

The Naval Academy Sailing Squadron (NASS) has become famous for the spinnakers on their forty-four-foot boats.
Courtesy of USNA

nerd nickel   Achievement pin from youngster YP cruise, different from the Navy's craftmaster pin.

net pay   What's left, usually dramatically less than a midshipman would like to have.

NFCU   Acronym for the Navy Federal Credit Union; the on-Yard bank where most midshipmen do their banking; NFCU has branches in most towns where there is a Navy base.

NFO   Acronym for naval flight officer, critical members of the many aviation communities except the helicopter community, where there are no NFOs.

ninth wing   Generically any apartment, apartment complex, or other housing used by recent Academy graduates on TAD while they await the beginning of their first service assignment; specifically, an apartment complex several miles from the Academy; also, the moment's most popular nightspot because it hosts many midshipmen or recent graduates. See also *DTA*.

NLT Acronym for not later than.

the nod (1) Affliction of sleepy midshipmen; most professors will allow midshipmen about to nod off to stand up in the back of the room and continue to take notes; see *touch and go(s)*. (2) Approval; the go-ahead ("Did LT Jones give you the nod?").

non-reg Short for non-regulation. See also *un-reg*.

NPQ Acronym for not physically qualified. See also *PQ*.

NPS (1) Acronym for Navy Postgraduate School, located in Monterey, California. (2) Acronym for nuclear power school, located in Charleston, South Carolina.

nuke Nickname for anyone in nuclear power, usually a submariner; an officer on a surface nuclear ship often is called a "surface nuke."

nuke it To give a much more complicated answer than necessary to a simple question; for example, for the question "What is 2 + 1?" a "nuke it" answer would be "$2 + 1 = \sqrt{9}$."

obligation Midshipman's service commitment; used often in reference to the number of contract years served in the Navy or Marine Corps following graduation; the obligation is five years following graduation except for certain communities (notably aviation) whose obligation is longer due to the length and cost of initial training.

ocean-e Short for the ocean engineering major, courses in it, or midshipmen majoring in it; some suggest that the "e" stands for "easy" and not engineering, making it "ocean easy."

O Club Short for the Officers' and Faculty Club; also, sometimes, the O&F club.

o-coat Four-button overcoat worn during cold weather over SDBs.

o course Short for the official Marine Corps obstacle course at the naval station.

office of legal counsel Office on the Yard that provides midshipmen with legal assistance and advice; in certain cases, the OLC counsel may act as the lawyer for, or defender of, a midshipman in discipline trouble; in such cases, a member of the department of leadership and law may act as an impartial investigator, provided the member of the OLC has not had the midshipman as a student.

"Oh Shit!" bridge Severn River bridge south of "Oh Shit!" hill.

"Oh Shit!" hill   First hill on Maryland Rt. 450 north of the Severn River bridge; it gets its name from the exclamation of some midshipmen as they crest the hill upon returning from liberty or leave, and see the Naval Academy before them.

OLC   Acronym for office of legal counsel.

on duty   Navy-wide term for a daily watch; for example, serving in one's company's rotational daily or weekly duty section.

1/C   Standard abbreviation for first class midshipman; also, 2/C denotes second class; 3/C, third class; 4/C, fourth class.

1MC   Pronounced "one-em-cee." Bancroft Hall speaker system, used for announcing formations, the weather, and uniforms for the day.

OOM   Acronym for order of merit.

"OO-RAH!"   Marine motivational call (or grunt); not to be confused with "HOO-YAH!"

OOW   Acronym for officer of the watch, a commissioned officer who is on duty on a particular day; stands with the MOOW, a midshipman.

order of merit   Class rank; a midshipman's relative standing in his or her class; a combination of academic, performance, conduct, and physical education standings; all grades are multiplied by predetermined coefficients, and the consequent numbers are totaled—resulting in an aggregate multiple.

O-Rep (or Fac Rep)   Short for Officer Representative (or Faculty Representative); an officer or civilian faculty member assigned to an athletic team or an extracurricular group (some teams have one of each); the team's or group's link(s) with the Academy administration.

ortho   Part of medical for (primarily) sports-related injuries.

outer   See inner.

overhead   Navy-wide term for any ceiling, or any lights in a ceiling; the underside of the above deck.

over the wall   Used variously with the verbs jump, hop, or go; the act of leaving (or entering) the Yard without permission; in the post–September 11th world, midshipmen actually jumping the wall may find themselves (1) in conduct trouble or (2) shot by Marine Corps guards believing them to be terrorists; not recommended anymore, not even for spirit-related events.

parades   A major part of Brigade life; there are formal parades on Worden Field and practice parades. See also *drill*.

Parents Weekend   At the end of Plebe Summer; frequently the first parental glimpse of a midshipman since I-Day; occasionally called Plebe Parents Weekend. See also *First Class Parents Weekend.*

passageway   Any hallway or corridor used for horizontal movement; commonly referred to as a "p-way."

pass in review   Part of formal parades when the Brigade marches before the reviewing officer(s); listening closely when "pass in review" is called, you might hear midshipmen whisper, "piss in your shoes."

PE   Acronym for physical education; all midshipmen must take PE each semester and must pass tests in the various required athletic activities.

peanut butter   On every table in King Hall, for every meal; some midshipmen subsist on it; there are both male and female varieties: male peanut butter is crunchy; female peanut butter is not.

PE deficient   Midshipman failing to meet any physical education standard is deemed PE deficient; he or she is assigned to a conditioning squad or subsquad where he or she works toward meeting the standard; those who do not meet it face separation.

pentagram   Nickname for the Pentagon.

PEP   Acronym for physical excellence program; taken during Plebe Summer; plebes sometimes call it the "plebe exhaustion program"; consists of early morning calisthenics on the Rip Miller Field and runs around the Yard; PEP is designed to elevate the physical condition of plebes to the standards of the Brigade.

pep rally   Mandatory fun, which usually isn't; sometimes the pep rallies are not planned in which case they are considered "spontaneous"; spontaneous pep rallies tend to be more fun.

performance   Evaluation of professional duties; a military ranking among the midshipmen within a company every semester; the ranking is determined by company firsties and ultimately the Company Officer; the grade is one included in a final OOM calculation.

Performance Board   Board that considers reported cases of substandard military performance by midshipmen.

performance grade   See *performance* and *OOM.*

phone home   An extremely seldom performed act inspired by the movie *E.T.;* regarding plebes, to get in the shower during Plebe Summer with one's clothes on and (for practice) to turn the shower knob in simulated dialing of a rotary telephone; now considered hazing and heavily prosecuted.

Plebes at PEP during Plebe Summer. PEP stands for the physical excellence program, but some midshipmen refer to it as the plebe exhaustion program.
Courtesy of USNA

phone room   Eradicated by the presence of phones in each Bancroft Hall room; previously, any of numerous pay telephone areas in Bancroft where midshipmen had to wait in line to call someone.

physical education   See *PE.*

physical readiness test   Navy-wide exercise that midshipmen must perform each semester; includes a one and one-half mile run, push-ups, sit-ups, and passage of the sit-and-reach flexibility test; almost always referred to as the *PRT.*

piece   Nonfunctioning, fused-bolt M-1 rifle used for drill.

pipe down   When used as a noun, means the completion of duty or watch activities. When used as a verb, means to go off duty.

pipeline   Likely future path within a warfare designation; the training schools a midshipman will attend after graduation, their location, etc. See also *career path.*

plate eater   Midshipman who simply cannot be filled at meals.

plates   Short for deckplates; metal squares on the floors of Bancroft Hall corridors at major chopping intersections where plebes turn, squaring their corners and sounding off; a common phrase; a take-off on a quote by World War II's Adm. Bull Halsey, "Hit the deckplates running; hit 'em hard, hit 'em fast, and hit 'em often."

platform   Navy-wide term for any surface ship, submarine, or aircraft used to launch ordnance.

platoon   Unit of organization within the Brigade; each company consists of four platoons; each platoon has three squads.

platoon commander   Two-striper midshipman in charge of a platoon.

plebe   From the word "plebian," meaning a commoner; in the modern vernacular, a low-life; a member of the fourth class at the Academy; the equivalent of a freshman at a civilian college (see *youngster, second class,* and *firstie*); at West Point, the fourth class are plebes; at the Air Force Academy they are doolies.

plebe cut   For men, shaved head; for women, short (above the collar). See also *hair.*

plebe detail   Contingent of upperclass, in either of two sets, assisting with training fourth class inductees during Plebe Summer; frequently shortened to "detail." See also *Joe.*

plebe hack   Cough most plebes get toward the end of Plebe Summer as a result of many things, persistent yelling among them; it spreads like wildfire, usually infecting most of the plebes.

plebe informal   A very occasional dance.

Plebe Parents Weekend   See *Parents Weekend.*

pleber   Nickname for a plebe.

plebe rate   Designated military or professional information a plebe is required to know.

Plebe Recognition Ceremony   See *Herndon.*

Plebe Summer   First midshipman ordeal, the beginning of the Naval Academy experience; a giant come-around. See also *real Plebe Summer.*

Plebe Summer smell/stench   Blended aroma of new uniforms, issue-gear, anxiety, and sweat; the smell unique to Plebe Summer and remembered by all midshipmen and Academy graduates.

plebette   A now seldom-used term for a female plebe.

plebe year   End of the beginning, officially concluded by the scaling of Herndon during Commissioning Week.

pledge   Another name for a plebe; akin to first-year counterparts in various fraternities and sororities nationwide.

POD   Pronounced "pee-oh-dee." Acronym for plan of the day; the posted bulletin of daily activities at the Academy and on the Yard, and giving notice of future events.

poli-sci and fly   Often-heard chant as to why someone decides to become a political science major; the sometimes accurate, sometimes imaginary claim is that the major is an easy one, allowing many who choose it to select aviation, usually a very sought-after job; Academy officials deny this claim, but political science usually is one of the most heavily subscribed majors at the Academy.

port-a-rack   Practice of flipping up the very stiff collar of a reefer while in class to allow for neck support and warmth while sleeping in class; not enjoyed by instructors and professors. See also *touch and go(s)* and *the nod.*

power squadron   Sarcastic reference to the Yard patrol (see *YP*) extracurricular activity (ECA), based on the unprovable supposition that it is filled with midshipmen who believe they are both (1) important and (2) powerful.

PQ   Acronym for physically qualified; a midshipman is either PQ or NPQ (not physically qualified), as determined primarily by precommissioning physicals called "precomms"; if a midshipman is designated NPQ, he or she cannot serve as an unrestricted line officer.

p-rade   Short for parade.

precomms   Short for precommissioning physicals for midshipmen; detailed and ongoing, they begin in the second semester of second class year and may continue until service assignment and/or graduation.

pre-registration   See *registration.*

presidential pardon   Tradition whereby the President of the United States, on visits to the Naval Academy, pardons all midshipmen on restriction at that time; in recent years, only minors have been pardoned; those with majors find themselves out of luck; also called "amnesty."

pretest   See *validate.*

Princess Leia   Motivational stunt pulled by plebes in which they cut a bread roll (hamburger bun, etc.) in half and slather each half with either peanut butter or mayonnaise; when a targeted upperclass is not looking, the plebe slaps the two halves on either side of the upperclass' head, hopefully causing them to stick; the ensuing image is akin to the hairstyle of Princess Leia in the first *Star Wars* film; tradition has it that if the plebe makes it up to his or her room without being caught by the upperclass, he or she is home free; if caught, however, the plebe's life will certainly become unpleasant; discouraged. See also *wildman.*

prior   Short for midshipmen who were enlisted prior to arriving as midshipmen; those who came to the Academy from the fleet or from the Marine Corps ("He's a prior").

probation   In most cases, an alternative to separation; restricted privileges, such as denial of weekends, because of deficiencies in academics, performance, conduct, or PE ("I'm on probation"); the message to midshipmen on probation: improve. See also *academic probation.*

pro book   paperback containing information on military subjects; used during plebe year so midshipman can become experts on myriad topics relating to the Navy and Marine Corps; signed periodically by upperclass to indicate that proper knowledge exists.

ProDev   Short for Division of Professional Development; the Academy division that co-ordinates professional training during the academic year, as well as summer training.

prof   Short for professor; the term used by midshipmen to refer to all Academy teachers.

professional   Adjectival near-synonym for "military" and/or "naval," as in "professional knowledge" or "professional development."

professional knowledge   Part of plebe training; information about military matters, ranging from uniforms to enemy armaments; "pro knowledge" also used. See also *pro topic.*

pro topic   Professional subject under study for a stipulated period (usually a week), during Plebe Summer and plebe year; such topics are delineated in plebe pro books, covered in plebe reference manuals, and tested in pro quizzes or pro tests (on Friday evenings, with makeups usually on Sundays). See also *professional knowledge.*

PROTRAMID   Acronym for professional training of midshipmen; in short, the time the Navy exposes midshipmen to (primarily) the aviation and submarine communities; usually takes place during second class summer; under significant revision at time of printing.

PRT   Acronym for physical readiness test.

PT   Acronym for physical training; any physical exercise—organized or unorganized ("I'm going out for some PT").

public affairs office The place to go at the Academy for answers.

puddle pirate Navy-wide nickname for a member of the U.S. Coast Guard.

punch out From the aviation phrase, meaning to eject; to separate or disenroll, that is, leave the Academy; also "to punch" ("He was having a tough time, so he punched").

punishment PT Physical exercise intended as a punishment; illegal. See also *SMT.*

p-way Short for passageway.

QPR Pronounced "kyooper." Acronym for quality point rating; the academic portion of *OOM;* QPRs can be semester or cumulative. See also *order of merit.*

rack When used as a noun, a bed. When used as a verb, to sleep.

rack attack Overwhelming need to sleep.

rack burn Temporary impression made on one's face by the "blue magnet," proof that one has recently been sleeping, usually restfully.

rack monster Mythical animal that grabs midshipmen and throws them into bed ("The rack monster got me!"); it can be a dangerous monster if it holds a mid hostage, especially causing him or her to miss a class; sometimes called a "rack-zilla" and a "rack-a-saurus."

rack option Right of plebes to go to bed at 10:00 PM.

rack races Plebe summer practices designed (1) to promote familiarity with making one's bed and (2) to promote speed in doing so. See also *uniform races.*

radar Process of a midshipman (usually a plebe) calling out bearings to cute girls along the road during march-overs to home football games ("Hottie at 2 o'clock").

rah Short for "OO-RAH"; sarcastic and usually said with the excitement of an earthworm.

rate When used as a noun, means designated military or professional information a plebe is required to know. When used as a verb, means to merit or qualify for; to be entitled to by class or rank ("Plebes do not rate that" or "You rate knowing this").

rate what you skate To do what you can get away with until you get caught.

ratey From the verb "to rate"; an adjective ordinarily employed in reference to plebes who enjoy privileges they are not normally permitted; for example, those who have longer hair, say "sir" too infrequently, or generally act insufficiently subordinate; an upperclass' observation might be, "Jones is ratey."

real Plebe Summer (or year)   Last tough one, usually the one experienced by the speaker.

recon   Spirit-promoting after-hours venture of plebes and (sometimes) upperclassmen; officially discouraged, especially with post–September 11th security measures. See also *over the wall.*

red beach   Any of the red-tiled areas at the back of Bancroft Hall and above King Hall where midshipmen catch rays, usually in un-reg gear; allowed under some administrations, forbidden under others. See also *green beach.*

reefer   Short three-button black winter coat for classes; the equivalent of a fleet p-coat; longer than an Ike jacket and shorter than an o-coat.

Reef Points   (1) Annually published manual for plebes since 1905. (2) From *Reef Points*, "pieces of small stuff used to reduce the area of a sail in strong winds, making for smoother sailing"; hence, helpful tidbits of information.

reform   Short for reformation; what happens when the entire Brigade returns from summer vacations and training and plebes occasionally are moved to different companies. See also *shuffling* and *shotgunning.*

reg hound   Slang term for any midshipman overly zealous in searching out violations of regulations. See also *Joe Mid, honor nazi,* and *reg nazi.*

regiment   One of two equally divided units of organization within the Brigade; first and second regiment (Note: during Plebe Summer, there is only one regiment: the fourth class regiment).

registration   Practice, beginning with pre-registration about one-third of the way through an existing semester, of scheduling one's courses for the next semester; about a month thereafter, during registration, every midshipman may find out his or her next-semester schedule from *MIDS;* among those things considered in drawing up schedules include required courses, requested classes and teachers, and availability.

reg nazi   See *reg hound.*

reg PE gear   Essentially blue shorts, blue-rim T-shirt, and (for plebes) issue socks pulled up as high as they can go. See also *blue rim.*

regs Short for regulations, from midshipman regulations (mid regs) as detailed in the *Midshipmen Regulations* (Mid Regs) publication ("What do the Regs say?" and "Look it up in the Regs").

resign To disenroll from the Academy. See also *separation.*

responses Five basic responses primarily intended for plebes but most are useful to each graduate throughout his or her career:

Yes, sir (or ma'am)

No, sir (or ma'am)

No excuse, sir (or ma'am)

I'll find out, sir (or ma'am)

Aye aye, sir (or ma'am)

restriction Serving of time for an infraction within the administrative conduct system; consists primarily of (1) personnel musters at least twice a day for uniform inspections, and (2) confinement to one's company area unless signed out for classes, library, or athletics; a midshipman on restriction may not go off the Yard; restriction is served by upperclass midshipmen over leave periods and may delay graduation if some restriction time remains; some believe inmates at minimum security prisons have more liberties. See also *head restrictee* and *Black N.*

retention Opposite of separation; a midshipman not separated is retained.

return of the Brigade Night at the end of Plebe Summer when upperclass return from summer training, and second class formally "introduce" themselves to plebes; sometimes referred to as "Hello Night," which is sometimes written "HELLo Night"; certainly not fun for plebes. See also *reform.*

reveille At 6:30 AM, proclaimed by the ringing of the bell and announced from the main office over the 1MC by an upperclass saying "Reveille, reveille. All hands heave out and trice up. Man the hatches with overheads lighted. Now reveille"; midshipmen are supposed to get out of bed at reveille (plebes must, upperclass occasionally do); the day's first obligation is a 7:00 AM formation that is then followed by breakfast.

reverse halo effect See *halo effect.*

RHIP Acronym for rank has its privileges; usually an expression of joy.

RHIR Acronym for rank has its responsibilities; usually an expression of resignation or frustration.

ride the goat   A plebe who has lost a bet to an upperclass must provide evidence (usually photographic) that he has ridden on the back of the bronze Bill the Goat statue while wearing either (1) nothing but skivvies or (2) nothing but a birthday suit; lately, midshipmen have also been riding the new submarine monument adjacent to Bancroft Hall's second wing, presenting an incredible sight; discouraged.

Ring Dance   Formal dance since 1925 that occurs at the end of second class year; second class hereafter are officially permitted to wear the class ring.

ring knocker   Midshipman or Academy graduate, especially one wearing the class ring; some argue that the first thing one learns about someone from Texas is that he or she is from Texas; the first thing one learns about a ring knocker is that he or she is an Academy graduate; the reciprocal supposition by the knocker is that some significant respect accordingly should be paid as a result; derogatory. See also *Joe Mid* and *cake-eater.*

road trip   Ordinarily to any nearby college, ordinarily to seek out the opposite sex. See also *hook up.*

rock   Midshipman who has extreme difficulty passing tests, such as tests in academics ("ac rock"), professional knowledge ("pro rock"), and swimming ("aqua rock").

the rocks   Large riprap on the Spa Creek seawall, frequently run on an outer.

roger   Navy-wide response meaning "yes" or "affirmative"; generically, often used with the word "that," for example, when answering "Are you taking a weekend?" the respondent says "Roger that."

room formal   See *inspections.*

rooming   Generally doubles and triples, with a few large rooms (barns) containing four or more; there are no singles; the genders are not mixed within rooms, but men's rooms and women's rooms are interspersed throughout Bancroft Hall; midshipmen may room only with members of the same company; rooms ordinarily are selected in the spring, by class, with firsties choosing first. See also *scramble.*

rumble   More physical form of "take out"; always plebes versus upperclass; illegal; also called "hall brawl."

run out   To do everything one can to force or drive another out of the Academy; illegal and severely prosecuted.

salty   Navy-wide adjective for someone who has a lot of Navy experience; someone who has been to sea many times can't help but be salty from all the sea air ("He's so salty").

Salty Sam   A now underground annually replaced anonymous columnist in *The Log,* who dishes dirt and sarcastically questions the dubious behavior of midshipmen and the administration. See also *The Log.*

saluting   Midshipmen salute all officers of the U.S. Armed Forces, plus officers of the U.S. Merchant Marine and the U.S. Public Health Service; those in the Navy and Marines salute with the right hand; contrary to those in the Army and Air Force, they may salute with the left if the right is encumbered; by custom, midshipmen sometimes salute midshipman acquaintances with dates on the Yard (see *left hand salute*); the rule for midshipmen is, when in doubt, salute.

sandblower   Slang for a short individual, the logic being that because of the given individual's vertical challenge, sand must be blown out of the way for him or her to breathe; usually, a midshipman marching in the back of his or her company during parades and march-overs.

sat   Short for satisfactory; acceptable academic average (see *CQPR, unsat,* and *gravy*) or in terms of military appearance or behavior.

sausage fest   Military-wide term used to describe any gathering in which the only occupants are men.

SAVI   Acronym for sexual assault victim intervention; from *Reef Points:* "provides sexual assault awareness and prevention education, victim advocacy, and data collection, while meeting the unique needs of sexual assault survivors in the Brigade."

scramble   To change, or mix, companies; two varieties: shuffling and shotgunning.

screen   Midshipman, usually a plebe, with mega "reverse halo effect"; a scapegoat; someone who attracts so much unwanted attention to himself or herself that others are "screened" from similar treatment; one who draws unusual attention to himself or herself and catches a lot of flak, often resulting in punishment. See also *shitscreen.*

screw the pooch   To do poorly ("I really screwed the pooch on that double E test"); also, if one does especially poorly (I "screwed the whole kennel").

scrounge   To look hard for, as in a midshipman scrounging in King Hall for extra slices of cheese.

SCUM   Acronym for a mythical and undocumented Academy group, the Society of Currently Unsat Midshipmen.

scuttlebutt   (1) Any drinking fountain. (2) Any rumor.

SDBs   Navy-wide acronym for service dress blues, the standard midshipman uniform for evenings, weekends, and off-campus wear during winter months. See also *uniforms.*

sea bag inspection   Inspection of a midshipman's issue gear, to make sure he or she has retained all of it; not a fun exercise.

SEAL   Acronym designating the Navy's sea, air, land special forces; a SEAL is a combination frogman/paratrooper/commando used for insertion, extraction, counterinsurgency, and reconnaissance; hence, a Navy commando. See also *BUD/S* and *Mini-BUD/S.*

sea lawyer   Midshipman, usually a plebe, who makes copious excuses, seldom taking responsibility for his or her actions, especially if punishment is involved or threatened.

seawall   Any reinforced water's edge on the Yard along the Severn River or along Spa or Dorsey Creeks.

second class   Member of the second class; the equivalent of a junior at a civilian college. See also *plebe, youngster,* and *firstie.*

second class alley   Any aisle between rows of tables where only members of the second class or first class may walk when going to and from tables in King Hall. See also *first class alley.*

second class entry   Either of two side entrances to Bancroft Hall's third and fourth wings from Tecumseh Court (T-Court).

second class loan   Popular name for a career starter loan; any of various loans offered to midshipmen at the end of second class year by various banks, and frequently accepted for purchases, for example, of a car. See also *midstang.*

section leader   Midshipman designated by the teacher, or volunteered by classmates, to take attendance in each class (not a glamorous job), a muster that is delivered to the instructor and reported for academic accountability on MIDS.

separation   Act of leaving the Academy for any reason whatsoever. See also *retention* and *sep pen.*

sep pen   Short for separation pending, meaning a midshipman whose separation from the Academy is awaiting administrative disposition; midshipman may, or may not, depart the Academy.

service assignment   (1) Act of being assigned one's community in the military. (2) Day (and night), usually in early spring of a firstie year, when firsties find out what they will be doing after graduation; a day of unspeakable joy or inconsolable lamentation.

sets   Two halves of Plebe Summer, called the first and second sets; upperclass in the plebe detail in charge of plebe training are different in each set.

Severn River hip disease   Sometimes imaginary weight gain phenomenon similar to the "freshman fifteen" that may afflict midshipmen of both sexes at the Academy as a result of the high-calorie content of food served in King Hall. See also *Hudson hips.*

sheet posters   Prepared seemingly without end by plebes for display inside and outside Bancroft Hall to promote Brigade spirit.

shipmate   Navy-wide term used to refer to anyone else in the Navy; sometimes used sarcastically by one midshipman toward another; for example, one roommate might say to another, "Hey, shipmate, could you hand me my toothbrush?"

Shipmate   Naval Academy's alumni magazine.

ships   Nickname for an advanced (and required) course in boats taken by naval architects.

Ships and Aircraft   Textbook issued to plebes containing fleet information on the subject matter.

shirtstays   Elastic straps connecting one's shirt-tail to one's socks to ensure proper tucked-in-ness; connected to a shirt on a hanger, they look like snakes that have bitten a shirt and are holding on for dear life; can prove quite an inconvenience to a midshipman experiencing bowel problems.

shitbag   Someone who does not do his or her job; not well liked.

shitscreen   Someone, usually a plebe, who attracts so much unwanted attention to himself or herself that others are screened from similar treatment. See also *screen.*

shoe   See *blackshoe.*

shotgunning   Mixing up plebes among all other companies; in this scrambling scenario, plebes are scattered throughout the Brigade and acquire a whole new group of company mates.

shoulder boards   Shoulder designations of rank.

shove off   (1) To leave, go away, often used in King Hall ("Shove off, scrounge"). (2) To be released from ("I got shoved off from a chow call").

shuffling Moving plebes together (as a group) from one company to another at reform; this variety of scrambling maintains the integrity of a company of plebes, sometimes helpful because returning youngsters do not have to join the ranks of those who recently "trained" them.

sick call One of a few designated periods during the day when midshipmen may go to medical with real or imagined afflictions.

the silent service Navy-wide term for the submarine community.

single E Slang for an English or economics major. See also *double E.*

SIR Acronym for sick in room; equivalent to fleet's SIQ (sick in quarters).

sir (ma'am) Appropriate form of address or response by any subordinate in conversation with a superior; plebes enter dangerous water if they confuse these two terms and address someone as the wrong gender, which happens frequently during the stresses of Plebe Summer.

six-N Dreaded day with six classes (the maximum) in a midshipman's academic schedule; five-Ns and four-Ns are tolerated better.

skate When used as a noun, means anything that is easy. When used as a verb, means to exert little effort ("I skated that class").

skivvies Navy-wide term for Navy-issue underdrawers or briefs.

slacker Midshipman who routinely performs far below his or her potential.

slayer Male midshipman who pathologically dates female midshipmen. See also *WL.*

slide Action taking place at the last muster of a sixty-day (or more) restriction period; two restrictees drag the now-former head restrictee the length of the rotunda, sliding his inspection-ready uniform along the floor through dust, signifying the end of *restriction.*

sliders Military-wide term for hamburgers. See also *Z burgers.*

slime When used as noun, means (1) disreputable individual or one possessing unflattering characteristics ("He turned me in, the slime") or (2) poor performance ("That's slime, plebe"). When used as a verb, means to turn sloppy or mushy corners as a plebe when corners should be properly squared ("He was sliming through the Hall").

smack Brown-noser, an apple-polisher, a kiss-ass; also used as a verb. See also *Joe Mid.*

smile (1) Curved indention in a properly rolled (and, when the curve is up, properly shelved) pair of socks. (2) Shape formed when the black elastic on a cover slips too low ("Fix your cover's smile"). (3) Band of dirt that sometimes forms on the white top of a midshipman's cover.

smoke   To do well (transitive) ("I smoked that test") or poorly (intransitive) ("I got smoked by that test").

SMT   Acronym for Saturday morning training; time reserved on Saturday mornings, which can begin very early in the dark hours, used to train plebes; activities often include long runs, swim PT, running the e-course, or any other creative activity (within the regs) that upperclass can conceive.

SNAFU   Military-wide acronym for situation normal, all f°°°ed up. See also *CF* and *FUBAR*.

snake   When used as a verb, means to take anybody else's anything, notably the date of another midshipman. When used as a noun, means one who takes something.

snake-eater   Military-wide nickname for a SEAL.

snarf   (1) To swipe or steal. (2) To eat quickly by large bites ("He snarfed down four pancakes in two minutes").

snipe   One serving in a ship's engineering department.

sock fishing   Practice of including an empty sock bag in one's laundry bag and having it mysteriously return with socks in it.

solitary confinement   Extreme kind of joke jail; solitary confinement is prescribed when a plebe's joke is exceptionally poor and the plebe must hold a spoon in front of his or her face instead of a fork.

SOP   Pronounced "ess-oh-pee." Military-wide acronym for standard operating procedure ("It's SOP; it's the way they do things around here").

sound off   To shout or yell; what plebes do when they square corners in Bancroft Hall.

spawning ground of the Navy   The U.S. Naval Academy, for two primary reasons: (1) the future leaders of the Navy and Marine Corps are trained there, and (2) many officers tend to have children while assigned there.

splashdown   Any dance, usually an impromptu one in a Bancroft hallway or basement, usually by plebes.

sponge   (1) Midshipman who easily soaks up knowledge. (2) Chronic borrower. (3) Something that easily (or intentionally) draws fire ("That frigate was a missile sponge for the carrier").

sponsors   The Academy's closest approximation of *in loco parentis*—hundreds of Annapolis area residents, many with Academy ties, who open their houses to midshipmen; every midshipman has a designated sponsor to whose house he or she may go when on liberty to hang out, let his or her hair down, or do whatever; sponsors frequently become counselors and confidants and friends, and are particularly helpful during plebe year; they are magnanimous and underpaid (they receive no stipend); in late fall, the Academy honors them with a weekend that includes special recognition and a dinner in King Hall.

spook Military-wide nickname for a spy or a member of the intelligence community. See also *intel.*

spoon When an upperclass officially tells a plebe his or her name ("I'm spooning you. Call me Steve"); to have that event happen to a plebe ("Mr. Jones spooned me today. He said to call him Steve"); discouraged by the administration because it implies a breakdown of the official plebe indoctrination system, especially if it occurs too early in the plebe year. See also *indoc.*

Sprint Nickname for the Navy lightweight football team, formerly known as 150s.

SQPR Pronounced "ess-kyooper." Acronym for semester quality point rating. See also *OOM* and *CQPR.*

squad Smallest unit of organization within the Brigade, generally consisting of about a dozen midshipmen; there are three squads in each platoon and twelve squads in each company.

squad leader A firstie; a one-striper billet, changed every semester.

squad tables See *tables.*

square corners To perform the plebe rite of making all turns in Bancroft hallways at ninety degrees while saying, "Go Navy, sir! Beat Army, sir!" (or "ma'am!"); an upperclass might say, "Plebe, square those corners!" See also *plates* and *sound off.*

square meal Motivational technique occurring occasionally in King Hall in connection with plebe training; the practice of moving one's utensils to and from the mouth at right angles; usually used as punishment; discouraged. See also *eat by the numbers.*

squid Nickname for midshipmen employed almost exclusively by cadets at the Air Force Academy and West Point; Naval Academy reciprocals for them are "zoomies" (Air Force) and "kaydets" or "woops" (West Point).

squid bait Term decreasing in use; akin to a "mid hound."

St. Andrew's Chapel The more intimate chapel under the main Academy chapel; used for smaller ceremonies and services.

star   To make the Superintendent's List, and thus to win the right to wear a gold star on the flap of the left breast pocket on certain uniforms (see *flare* and *Joe pins*); also, sometimes, to make the Dean's List and thus to win the right to wear a bronze star; when used as a noun, the stars themselves.

station   Navy-wide term for any place where one serves duty. See also *duty station.*

steam   Required engineering course, generally thermodynamics for non–group I majors.

Steerage   Restaurant in Bancroft Hall for midshipmen (nights only); between third and fourth wings, adjacent to Smoke Hall. See also *Drydock.*

St. John's College   Third-oldest school in the nation; a remarkable liberal arts college and graduate program that happens to be a collegiate croquet power (one of the country's few); located across the street from the Naval Academy.

stoked   Term decreasing in use; means really pumped up, excited, or prepared ("I'm really stoked for the game").

storage   Generally, the mandatory storing of personal items, including computers, somewhere in Bancroft Hall during summer vacation.

striper   Term that invariably carries with it negative connotations; any midshipman officer who is (1) a first class with rank in the company or in the Brigade, so designated by the stripes on his or her shoulder boards and sleeves; usually a three striper or above; a mega (or super) striper is one with four, five, or six stripes; the stripes have name equivalents to rank in the fleet; in both semesters only rarely will a firstie besides a Brigade commander wear a total exceeding six stripes (e.g., if two in the first semester then no more than four in the second); or (2) a midshipman in the striper organizational network of any of the other three classes.

striper billet   Position designated or held in a striper chain of command.

striper dick   Striper whose position has gone to his or her head; one who uses his or her power to an excessive degree. See also *Joe.*

struggling   Used either as a noun or adjective; midshipman (of either sex) who is less than attractive ("That guy is struggling" or "Did you see that struggling guy back there?").

sub squad   Special-regime group for those having trouble with any failed PE class; most often used regarding swimming failures. See also *PE deficient.*

suck it up   To accept a situation—usually a tough one; to buckle down and deal with it ("With four tests and two papers next week, you'll just have to suck it up" or "You got a major for going over the wall; suck it up, bro"); the phrase related to the adage, "If you're gonna be dumb, you gotta be tough."

summer elective training   Any of many possible optional cruise blocks. See also *summer training.*

summer school   Some courses are taught at the Academy during the summer for makeup and enrichment.

summer seminar   Any of three one-week sessions that take place each summer at the Naval Academy; the primary purpose of summer seminar is to expose high school kids (who are already performing well academically) to the Academy and its nuances; seminar is competitive: seven thousand apply and only eighteen hundred attend, with only six hundred per week; rising youngsters serve as *detailers* for the students, but act more like counselors; there exists almost no yelling so the experience is overwhelmingly a positive one; a huge recruiting tool for the Academy.

summer training   Way midshipmen spend their summers; following Commissioning Week (and sometimes prior to it), all midshipmen in the three remaining classes have leave or some form of summer training. See also *blocks* and *summer elective training.*

summer whites   The summer equivalent of SDBs. See also *ice cream suit* and *uniforms.*

Supe   See *Superintendent.*

Superintendent   Individual in charge; the highest-ranking official at the Naval Academy.

Superintendent's List   Made by about 6 percent of midshipmen; requirements are semester QPR of at least 3.4 with no semester grades below a C, an A in military performance, an A in conduct, at least a B in physical education; those qualifying may wear a gold star on certain uniforms.

Supe's List   See *Superintendent's List.*

surface nuke   Nuclear trained officer who also drives ships. See also *nuke.*

swarrior   Generally sarcastic nickname for a surface warfare officer. See also *SWO.*

sweat   When used as a noun, means midshipman who worries about everything ("He's a sweat"). When used as a verb, means to worry excessively ("Don't sweat it").

sweet Widely used expression meaning excellent, great, cool, terrific, etc.

SWO (1) Acronym for a surface warfare officer. (2) The surface warfare community, that is, the surface Navy ("I'm going SWO").

SWO-daddy Navy-wide nickname for a surface warfare officer.

SWOnut Slang term for a doughnut, the suggestion being that like police officers, SWOs live for the things—an addiction sometimes visible in waistlines. See also *cake-eater.*

SWOtivator (1) A perhaps overly motivated firstie who will be a surface warfare officer following graduation. (2) A SWO at the Academy who tries to recruit midshipmen for the surface community.

systems Short for the systems engineering major that combines electrical, mechanical, control, and computer engineering; usually the largest group I major and a top (usually the number one) such program in the country.

tables Short for squad tables; the regular arrangement for dining in King Hall; frequently used in the phrase "at tables" ("We were at tables, and he dropped the tray" or "Are you going down to tables?"). See also *team tables* and *hot seat.*

tac Military jargon for a hyphen.

TACAMO Acronym for take charge and move out.

TAD Pronounced "tee-ay-dee." Acronym for temporary assigned duty; at the Academy, the duty served between graduation and a graduate's first duty station; duty is "temporary" because it normally lasts less than six months; duty longer than six months ordinarily is defined as a permanent change of station (PCS).

tailgating Where all the fun is at football games; a post- (or during-) event tradition that takes place in the parking lots at certain sports contests, notably football, lacrosse, and crew.

take out Term borrowed from the mafia, meaning to "get" an upperclass, usually in some organized fashion (unlike the mafia, however, no one is killed); to harass an upperclass mildly, for example, with shaving cream, and often during rumbles or hall brawls; illegal and feverishly prosecuted by the administration.

tango company During Plebe Summer, for those who want to leave the Academy; departing midshipmen live in tango company as they are processing out of the Academy, which is a very involved process that usually takes a great deal of time.

tape off To remove the lint from one's uniform with a whisk broom or tape, as in one roommate saying to another, "Hey, quick, tape me off."

taps   Time when midshipmen must be in their company area for an accountability muster; not being there generally means a future fry; specific times vary depending on the current administration. See also *lights out* and *touch and go(s)*.

TBS   Acronym for The Basic School in Quantico, Virginia; the first place Marine Corps officers go.

T-Court   Short for Tecumseh Court; in front of Bancroft Hall; name taken from the nearby bronze statue that is called "Tecumseh."

teacher/instructor evals   Forms, filled out at the end of each semester prior to exams, on which midshipmen write their opinions of their teachers; the forms are read by both the teacher and by his or her department chairman following the issuance of final grades; midshipmen have the option of signing their name or submitting the form anonymously; also called "get back sheets" and "slam sheets."

team tables   As opposed to squad tables (see *tables*), meal tables for in-season varsity athletes; designed to promote team unity in a nonathletic environment, and to accommodate irregular practice times ("We've got late tables tonight"); in accordance with National Collegiate Athletic Association (NCAA) rules, no special food is served.

Tecumseh   Bronze statue of Tamanend, a peaceful Delaware chief; long ago midshipmen nicknamed statue "Tecumseh," after the war-loving Shawnee chief; frequently called the "God of 2.0" (see *unsat*); some midshipmen toss pennies at Tecumseh en route to their exams for good luck, trying to get the pennies in his quiver (which, by the way, is solid). See also *T-Court*.

telephone   Phones are in every Bancroft Hall room; they are the main link with the outside; all of them have voice mail; the only thing perhaps more reliable is e-mail.

ten-meter board   Diving platform, close to the ceiling of Lejeune Hall, from which all midshipmen must jump prior to graduation; failure to jump may lead to separation; also called "the ten-meter tower."

Thanksgiving rule   A sometimes mythical, sometimes true dictum holding that a plebe with a steady girlfriend or boyfriend prior to I-Day will lose that relationship by Thanksgiving. See also *2% Club*.

thermo   Short for courses in thermodynamics.

three chews and a swallow   Motivational technique (now forbidden) during Plebe Summer in connection with plebe training; the intent is to "encourage" plebes to take small bites of food in command situations so their mouths will never be stuffed; now contrary to plebe indoctrination. See also *indoc.*

tool   A jerk. See also *Joe Mid.*

touch and go(s)   (1) From the aviation phrase meaning to practice take-offs and landings; the affliction of chronically tired midshipmen trying to stay awake in class; the head nods forward, slowly at first, then more quickly, ultimately waking the midshipman up; after straightening his or her head, the process begins again; also called "the nod." (2) Practice of coming back to the Yard for taps, then jumping the wall to go back out; illegal and an honor offense.

tour   (1) Disciplinary punishment wherein the guilty party marches hour-long segments on weekends or holidays in an area so designated for each battalion, either outside or inside, and usually beginning very early in the morning (0530); an alternative punishment to restriction. (2) Navy-wide term for a billet or duty station; those in the Navy usually will alternate between sea tours and shore tours.

tower   See *ten-meter board.*

townie   Individual who dwells in Crabtown (Annapolis). See also *mid hound.*

town liberty   Liberty within the vicinity of Annapolis and the Naval Academy; specifics vary according to current administrations. See also *liberty, Yard liberty,* and *leave.*

training time out   What someone calls if he or she feels training is either (1) too tough, (2) too confusing, or (3) if there exists the possibility for someone to get hurt; in essence, a safety measure.

The Trident   Weekly tabloid newspaper produced by the Academy's public affairs office; it appears on Fridays forty-nine times per year, and is also available by subscription.

Trident scholar   One of the smartest (academically) midshipmen; a few brainy firsties authorized to take a reduced class load in order to complete a major research project. See also *dork fork.*

Triton Light   Monument at the corner of the Yard where the Severn River and Spa Creek seawalls join; a gift from the class of 1954, it is probably the only navigational light in the world that blinks five times, then four times, then five, then four, and so on.

trucker's English Slang for a lower-level course in English for a small number of plebes; the term is not sanctioned by Academy administration officials but is used insistently by both trucker's students and English department faculty; not intended as a derogatory term, simply a descriptive one.

trucker's meal Any meal eaten in King Hall in which the eater uses no utensils and must therefore eat only with his or her hands; sometimes a trucker's meal also entails the eaters turning their chairs around, rolling up their sleeves, and eating with elbows on the table; sometimes motivated by the entree itself—chicken-fried steak with mashed potatoes and gravy; performed only periodically due to its "unprofessional" nature.

tuck When used as a noun, means a fold in the back of a uniform's shirt to give it a neat appearance. When used as a verb, means to make such a fold or crease.

two for seven Point of no return; point that is passed when second class enter their first class in the fall of second class year; thereby, they agree to two more years at the Academy plus a five-year minimum service obligation following graduation.

two-inch bulk rule Regulation that for female midshipmen, the volume (or mass) of the hair may not extend up or out more than two inches from the head.

2% Club Nondocumented group whose members are those midshipmen—purportedly 2 percent of those with steady dating relationships begun prior to I-Day—whose relationships survive until graduation and beyond. See also *Thanksgiving rule.*

2.0 and go Pronounced "two-point-oh and go." Phrase referring to the GPA necessary for graduation, the suggestion on the part of some being, "Who cares what my grades are as long as I graduate?"

UA Military-wide acronym for unauthorized absence; another way of saying AWOL.

uncover To remove one's cover (or any hat) when going inside.

underclass Any midshipman who is not a firstie; not used as frequently as the term "upperclass."

uniform races Plebe Summer practices designed (1) to promote familiarity with the Navy uniform and (2) to teach speed in getting in and out of it. See also *rack races.*

uniforms During the academic day, midshipmen wear working uniforms; outside the Yard they wear either summer whites or SDBs, depending on the weather; numerous other uniforms exist for special and/or dressy occasions, among them are khakis, chokers, FDBs, and whiteworks.

un-reg   Any action, behavior, procedure, condition, or attire contrary to regulations. See also *non-reg.*

unsat   (1) Short for unsatisfactory in terms of dress or behavior ("That's unsat, Mister"). (2) Condition of either having an academic average below 2.0 or having an F (or two Ds). See also *academically deficient, order of merit,* and *sat.*

upperclass   Any midshipman except a plebe ("He's an upperclass"). See also *underclass.*

USAA   Acronym for United Services Automobile Association; an insurance company and bank used by many midshipmen; known for superlative customer service.

using my honor against me   Phrase midshipman might use when feeling he or she is in a situation in which information is being wrongly demanded; for example, if asked, "Did you break any rules this weekend?" a midshipman could suggest that "a reply would be using my honor against me"; this phrase is intended to be an Academy approximation of the U.S. Constitution's Fifth Amendment defense against self-incrimination.

validate   Generally, to test out of; to get academic credit for, particularly as an incoming plebe; to perform outstandingly on a PE test before the scheduled beginning of that PE segment.

VGEP   Acronym for volunteer graduate education program, a competitive program open to midshipmen highly proficient in academics; under VGEP, in their second semester firsties may take courses toward Masters degrees at any of a number of nearby colleges, generally with completion of the degree program by the end of the calendar year in which they graduate from the Academy.

visitor center   Where tourists go; few midshipmen do.

walk-through   See *inspections.*

the wall   (1) Structure separating the Yard from the rest of the world; see *over the wall.* (2) Fifty-foot tall indoor rock climbing facility in the back of Halsey Field House.

wanna-be   Someone who wants too desperately to become something, and frequently acts that way ("He's a Marine wanna-be").

wardroom   Short for company wardroom.

warfare designation pin   Piece of gold worn on an officer's chest signifying his or her warfare community: aviation wings, SEAL trident, SWO pin, etc.

warfare specialty schools   Places new Academy graduates go to be trained in various elements of warfighting.

watch   Duty of all midshipmen and most Navy personnel; an obligation in Bancroft Hall consisting of rotating watch duties, for example, CDO, CMOD, MOM, OOW, and BOOW.

water skiing   Practice of having each bare foot placed in its own urinal and flushing, again, and again; considered hazing.

water wings   Slang for the surface warfare breast insignia.

weekend eligible   Midshipmen may not be eligible to take weekends (that is, they may be non–weekend eligible) if they (1) have a QPR below 2.0 (see *academically deficient*), (2) are on restriction, (3) are on any kind of probation, or (4) have any deficiency or are on any sub squad.

West Point   Commonly used term for the U.S. Military Academy in Highland Falls, New York; its class designations—in order—are plebe, yearling, cow, and firstie. See also *classes* and *Air Force Academy.*

whatever flips your skirt   Phrase said in response to a statement about any preference ("You like to study with the windows open in the winter? Whatever flips your skirt"); "Whatever floats your boat" also used.

whiskey lima   See *WL* and *slayer.*

whites   Short for summer whites. See also *uniforms.*

whiteworks challenge   Midshipmen are only allowed to wear the (comparatively comfortable) whiteworks uniform on days when they have an actual PE class; the challenge is for people to try to wear whiteworks for an entire week without being caught and fried; the difference in comfort is apparently worth the risk. See also *uniforms.*

wildman   Motivational stunt pulled by plebes in King Hall in which they throw some liquid (usually a full pitcher of water) at an unsuspecting upperclass. Tradition has it that if the plebe makes it up to his or her room without being caught by the upperclass, he or she is home free; if caught, however, the plebe's life will certainly become unpleasant. See also *assassination* and *Princess Leia.*

wingman   (1) Taken from the aviation term; one's constant companion, strongest supporter, or closest confidant ("My roommates are great but so-and-so is my wingman"). (2) Companion who accompanies you out to bars/clubs, willing to talk to companions of people you may want to "hook up" with.

wings (1) Pilot's wings, jump wings, etc. (2) Slang term for the female uniform necktie. (3) Eight primary sections of Bancroft Hall; each consists of five floors (or decks) for living, plus two basement levels; numbering of the living floors is 0 through 4; midshipmen discussing where they live will commonly cite their wing and their floor—in that order, for example, midshipman living on 5-0 resides in the fifth wing on the zero deck (the first residential floor), a midshipman living on 6-2 resides in the sixth wing on the second deck (the third residential floor).

wires Level of electrical engineering taken by non-engineering majors. See also *cables.*

WL From the phonetic alphabet, whiskey lima, acronym stands for "WUBA lover"; the term refers to a male midshipman who dates female midshipmen; very derogatory. See also *WUBA.*

woop Midshipmen nickname for cadets at West Point; taken after the noise of the flying monkeys in the film *The Wizard of Oz* because the monkeys wore capes similar to the capes integral to the West Point uniform. See also *squid.*

word Military-wide term for information ("Pass the word").

WRNV Midshipman-run FM radio station, complete with midshipmen disc jockeys; located in the basement of Bancroft Halls's eighth wing; by contrast, WNAV is an AM commercial station in Annapolis.

W. T. Door Former term for a generic or typical midshipman; legend has it that he roomed with Joe Gish and that the two lived next to the Company Officer; popular belief is that these two dorks finally graduated because there is so little reference to them anymore; they have been replaced by a seemingly endless supply of Joe Mids.

WUBA Pronounced "wooba," rhyming with tuba. Incredibly derogatory term abhorred by Academy officials; used to describe female midshipmen; as an acronym, WUBA stands for many things, the only one acceptable enough to print, however, is "women with unusually bad attitudes"; term came about due to a particular kind of uniform midshipmen wear: working uniform blue alpha (WUBAs); same uniform is still worn, but is now called winter working blues (WWBs).

WWBs Acronym for winter working blues, the standard midshipman class day uniform during winter months. See also *uniforms.*

X-period   Period before first period that occurs six and twelve weeks into the semester, used primarily for exams. See also *X-week*.

X-week   Week six and week twelve of each semester; week is altered by adding X-periods in the morning for exams.

yankee bravo   Derogatory term, taken from the phonetic alphabet abbreviation YB, for "your boy," a suggestion that someone who may be acting like a dork or a Joe is close friends with someone else who is not ("I hear yankee bravo fried my roommate for sleeping two minutes late").

the Yard   The U.S. Naval Academy campus.

Yard liberty   Liberty anywhere on, but restricted to, the Yard. See also *liberty, town liberty,* and *leave.*

Yard mail   Mail among Academy buildings; similar to a civilian company's inter-office mail.

youngster   (1) Member of the third class; the equivalent of a sophomore at a civilian college; see *plebe, second class,* and *firstie.* (2) Day when a midshipman has no classes after lunch (i.e., during fifth and sixth periods); see *civilian.*

youngster bridge(s)/walkway(s)   Low walls along the sidewalks on either side of Chauvenet and Michelson Halls, saving their users the apparent inconvenience of walking down four steps, then some forty paces later, up four steps; not for use by plebes.

youngster cruise   Part of required summer training for rising youngsters, consisting of at least a YP cruise and one other block of training.

youngster ladder   Any Bancroft Hall stairway narrow enough that the extended arms can touch both walls; not for use by plebes.

youngster summer   See *youngster cruise.*

YP   Acronym for yard patrol craft; any of several 108-foot-long boats stationed at the Academy; often used in conjunction with professional, leadership, and navigational courses, as well as for summer training.

"yut"   Sarcastic "OORAH!" See also *rah.*

yut cut   Sarcastic reference to a perhaps overly motivated very short haircut, usually a "high and tight."

Z burgers   Naval Academy hamburgers; so named for their alleged power to induce sleep (Zs) in those who eat them, particularly in those who eat them at lunch and then go to fifth or sixth period classes. See also *sliders.*

zero dark thirty   Early; when many midshipmen awaken each morning, in the dark, primarily in the winter.

zoomie   Midshipmen nickname for cadets at the Air Force Academy. See also *squid*.

The future of the U.S. Naval Academy? A boy in regulation midshipman physical education (PE) gear awaits the passing of the Brigade during march-on to a home football game.
Courtesy of USNA

The U.S. Naval Academy crest or seal.

Courtesy of USNA

Appendix:
Internet Resources

Web site information appears throughout the text of *Brief Points*. Following is a listing of the Web site addresses mentioned in the book. The addresses have been grouped alphabetically by subject for ease of reference.

Airports

Baltimore-Washington International Airport:

www.bwiairport.com

Dulles International Airport:

www.metwashairports.com/Dulles

Ronald Reagan Washington National Airport:

www.metwashairports.com/National/Index.html

Annapolis

Annapolis and Anne Arundel County Chamber of Commerce:

www.annapolischamber.com

City of Annapolis:

www.ci.annapolis.md.us

Annapolis Visitors Bureau:

www.visit-annapolis.org

Boat Shows

Information on powerboat and sailboat shows held in Annapolis each fall:

www.usboat.com

Career Opportunities for Midshipmen

Naval Academy Catalog:

www.usna.edu/Catalog/career.pdf

A good place to start when considering opportunities for midshipmen after they have been commissioned.

Naval Aviation

National Naval Aviation Museum, Pensacola, Florida:

www.naval-air.org

SEALs

https://www.seal.navy.mil

Special Operations

www.bupers.navy.mil/pers2/specops/specopsnew.htm

Submarines

www.chinfo.navy.mil/navpalib/cno/n87/n77.html

Surface Warfare

USNA Division of Professional Development's Web site for prospective surface warfare officers:

http://prodevweb.prodev.usna.edu/SWO/swocip.htm

Provides very good information on service assignment.

U.S. Navy's official Web site for surface warfare officers:

https://www.swonet.com/cgi-bin/swoprod.dll/public.jsp

U.S. Marine Corps

www.usmc.mil

U.S. Navy

www.navy.mil

Class Rings

Herff Jones:

www.herff-jones.com

Jostens:

www.jostens.com

Military Money

Defense Financing and Accounting Service:

www.dfas.mil/money/milpay

Many officers bookmark this site because it answers in detail the myriad questions they (and their families) have regarding pay issues.

Military Leave and Earnings Statement:

www.dfas.mil/money/milpay/les_djms.pdf

Naval Academy Prep School (NAPS)

www.naps.edu

Navy Uniform Regulations

Bureau of Naval Personnel:

www.bupers.navy.mil/uniform/uniform.html

U.S. Navy Uniform Regulations:

buperscd.technology.navy.mil/bup_updt/508/unireg/uregMenu.html

Includes grooming standards, uniform components, and rank insignia.

Local Newspapers

Trident:

www.dcmilitary.com/navy/trident

The [Annapolis] Capital:

www.hometownannapolis.com

The Baltimore Sun:

www.sunspot.net

The Washington Post:

www.washingtonpost.com

The Washington Times:

www.washtimes.com

Service Academies

U.S. Air Force Academy:

www.usafa.af.mil

U.S. Coast Guard Academy:

www.cga.edu

U.S. Merchant Marine Academy:

www.usmma.edu

U.S. Military Academy (West Point):

www.usma.edu

U.S. Naval Academy:

www.usna.edu

Local Travel

AMTRAK:

www.amtrak.com

Maryland Transit Authority:

www.mtamaryland.com/index.cfm

Omega World Travel:

www.owt.net

Has an office in Bancroft Hall's third wing basement.

Washington Metropolitan Area Transit Authority:

www.wmata.com/default.cfm

U.S. Naval Academy

Academic Courses

www.usna.edu/acdean/courses/courses.html

Provides links to each academic department's course offerings with a brief description of each course, credits, schedule, and any prerequisites.

Academic Dean and Provost

www.nadn.navy.mil/AcDean/staff/staff.html

Academics

www.usna.edu/acdean

Provides links to schedules, academic programs, courses, officer faculty opportunities, and much more.

Administrative Links

www.usna.edu/admin.htm

Admissions

www.usna.edu/Admissions

Nominations:

www.usna.edu/Admissions/steps4.htm

Provides references, lists of political nomination sources, and admissions requirements.

Alumni Association and Foundation

www.usna.com

Athletics

Navy intercollegiate, intramural, and club sports:

www.usna.edu/athletics.htm

Navy intercollegiate sports only:

www.navysports.com

Catalog

www.usna.edu/Catalog

Character Development

www.usna.edu/CharacterDevelopment/homepage.html

Club Sports

www.usna.edu/athletics.htm

www.usna.edu/PEScheds/clubhome.htm

Commandant of Midshipmen

www.usna.edu/Commandant

Distinguished Artist Series

www.usna.edu/Music/distartseries.html

Drydock Restaurant, Dahlgren Hall

www.usna.edu/NAF/DryDock

Graduate Education

www.usna.edu/GraduateEducation

History

www.usna.edu/VirtualTour/150years

Honor

www.usna.edu/CharacterDevelopment/honor/honor_index.html

Midshipmen Activities

www.usna.edu/MidActivities/activity.html

Museum

www.usna.edu/Museum

Naval Academy Foreign Affairs Conference

www.usna.edu/NAFAC

Naval Station Annapolis

www.usna.edu/NavalStation/newpage.htm

Officers' and Faculty Club

www.usna.edu/MWR/club.htm

Parents' Organizations

Naval Academy Alumni Association's list:

http://usna.com/Communities/parents/parents/htm

USNA-Net

www.usna-net.org

This rapidly growing parents' Web site has everything from a parent's handbook to archives of frequently asked questions.

Important Phone Numbers

www.usna.edu/PAO/phone.htm

Public Affairs Office

www.usna.edu/PAO

Running Routes

www.usna.edu/PEScheds/running_routes.pdf

Schedules

Academy and some local events:

www.usna.edu/PAO/calendars.htm

Generic daily midshipman schedule:

www.usna.edu/schedule.htm

Shoulder Boards

www.usna-net.org/handbook/summer.html#boards

Superintendent

www.usna.edu/PAO/supesoff.html

Tickets

Tickets for athletic events:

www.navysports.com/info/tickets

Tickets for Academy functions:

www.tickets.com

Twenty-Two Mile Limit

www.usna-net.org/handbook/22mile.html

Also provides a link to a high-resolution map showing the area in much greater detail.

WRNV

www.usna.edu/WRNV

U.S. Naval Institute and the Naval Institute Press

www.navalinstitute.org

Visiting USNA

Annapolis Tours:

www.annapolis-tours.com

Provides walking tours with a historical view of the city that includes the Naval Academy.

Naval Academy tours and online shopping:

www.navyonline.com

Index

About the Author

Ross H. Mackenzie graduated from the U.S. Naval Academy in 1994 with a B.S. in English. He is a naval aviator who flies the SH-60B (Seahawk) helicopter (pictured below). He has been on numerous deployments with the U.S. Navy—both short and long—everywhere from the Caribbean to the Gulf of Alaska and from the Eastern Pacific to the Persian Gulf.

While teaching English literature and writing at the Naval Academy, Mackenzie earned his M.A. in liberal arts from St. John's College in Annapolis. He makes his home in Florida with his wife, Elizabeth, and two children. He also writes short fiction and children's literature.